Better Homes and Gardens®

Cabinets & Shelves

WILEY

John Wiley & Sons, Inc.

For general information about our other products and services, please contact our Customer Care Department within the United States at (800) 762-2974, outside the United States at (317) 572-3993 or fax (317) 572-4002.

Wiley also publishes its books in a variety of electronic formats. Some content that appears in print may not be available in electronic books. For more information about Wiley products, visit our web site at www.wiley.com.

ISBN 978-0-696-23297-8

Printed in the United States of America

10 9 8 7 6

Note to the Readers:
Due to differing conditions, tools, and individual skills, John Wiley & Sons, Inc., assumes no responsibility for any damages, injuries suffered, or losses incurred as a result of following the information published in this book. Before beginning any project, review the instructions carefully, and if any doubts or questions remain, consult local experts or authorities. Because codes and regulations vary greatly, you always should check with authorities to ensure that your project complies with all applicable local codes and regulations. Always read and observe all of the safety precautions provided by manufacturers of any tools, equipment, or supplies, and follow all accepted safety procedures.

Table of Contents

Introduction

Cabinets, shelves, and storage units are mostly simple carpentry projects that almost anyone can accomplish. Sturdy, basic open storage shelves for a garage or basement can be built quickly with readily available hardware using basic tools. Most large home centers and lumberyards will even cut sheets of plywood or other materials to size for a nominal charge, making your job even simpler.

If you want to build any kind of storage unit, from basic basement utility shelving to bookcases and other units for living areas in the home, this book is for you. If you just want to hang a shelf on a wall to hold your favorite knickknack, put up some adjustable shelf standards for bookshelves, or make some places to set potted plants, start with pages 12–17 for a look at some simple shelves. Many of these can be installed in just a few hours.

In the chapter about kitchen cabinets, beginning on page 34, you'll learn how to lay out cabinets for an efficient kitchen. The chapter also discusses the types of cabinets available and how to install factory-made cabinets that you can buy at any home center. With a little time and care, you can build your own cabinets from instructions in the chapter.

Chapter 4 (pages 78–93) introduces you to the materials and tools you can use to construct shelving and storage projects. In many cases, you will already have many of the tools you need for a project. The skills and carpentry techniques you'll need to put your project together are discussed in chapter 5 (pages 94–121). From measuring and marking to cutting parts and assembling them, this chapter will answer most of your questions about building projects.

On pages 60–77 you'll find instructions for a variety of projects ranging from bookcases and an entertainment center to a wine rack. Designed to be simple to build, sturdy, and attractive, these projects can be used as the basis for your own designs.

Building or installing shelves is the first excursion into home improvement for many people. While a task like hanging a shelf on a wall seems simple at first glance, there are many planning considerations and details that make it more complicated. And as the project moves beyond one simple shelf, the complexity increases. But the good news is that these projects proceed logically and rely on basic skills, so you can accomplish a project of any size by following a straightforward, step-by-step approach.

The first step in any storage or shelving project is to determine what you need to accomplish. Whether your goal is to hang up one shelf on a dining room wall for a tea set or to build shelves for boxes in the basement, start with a rough sketch of the project. The sketch doesn't need to show details, just the rough shape.

Show dimensions on the sketch to make sure the unit will meet the need and will fit the space you have available. Take into account the size and amount of stuff you want to put on the shelf or shelves. Consider the weight: A shelf for a tea set won't need to be as substantial as a shelf for hardbound books.

Think about the appearance of the finished project. Shelves in an unfinished basement storage room can be made of construction lumber, nailed together with galvanized metal hardware, and painted. In the living room or family room, bookcases and shelves should be made of better-looking wood—perhaps hardwoods—with more attractive joinery. The shelves might be painted or stained and given a clear finish.

Consider the tools and skills you have available for the job. A cordless electric drill/driver, a tape measure, a level, and a handsaw or jigsaw will probably be adequate for putting up a simple shelf. And you can do the job with a few carpentry skills within an hour or two. You can do most of the work right in the room where you're putting the shelf—but cover the floor if you're in the living area of the house.

More ambitious projects such as a bookcase or entertainment center will take more time. You'll probably need more tools too; a portable circular saw or a tablesaw will make a larger project easier. You might need a router to make joints. And you'll need the skills to use these tools, but they're just extensions of your basic skills and easy to learn.

It's better to set up a work area in a corner of the basement or garage for a larger project so you can work on it without disrupting life in the rest of the house. It might take you several nights and weekends to construct a bookcase.

Start with simple projects to build your confidence and skills. Then progress to more complex jobs as you become a more adept do-it-yourselfer.

How to use this book

Start by browsing through the gallery of photos for ideas, then look through projects until you find one that will accomplish your shelving and storage goals. Study the project to get an idea of how it goes together. In many cases you can adapt a project from the book to meet specific needs by making minor changes.

If the project calls for materials, tools, or skills that aren't familiar to you, refer to the last two chapters in the book for more information. Materials and tools are discussed in chapter 4 beginning on page 78; carpentry skills and techniques are covered in chapter 5 beginning on page 94.

If a technique is new to you, practice on scrap lumber before you cut into the boards you buy for the project. The same goes for a new tool; become familiar with how to use it and practice with it before you start the project. You can usually rent a power tool instead of buying it. Ask the rental dealer to show you how to use the tool before you take it home.

Make a shopping list for the lumber and hardware you'll need. Lumber is sold in standard lengths, 2-foot increments, usually beginning at 6 or 8 feet long, so you will have to cut your project parts from longer pieces in most cases. Many lumberyards and home centers will cut lumber to length for a nominal charge. As you cut the parts, label them.

Be sure you understand the instructions and how the project goes together before you start cutting and assembling the parts. Planning ahead always prevents frustration and saves time and money.

Look for these helpers

You'll find these boxes with tips and hints throughout the book. Used with the instructions, they will help you complete your project safely and efficiently.

You'll Need

To help you plan the job, this box lists the major tools and some of the principal skills you'll need to complete a project. It also includes an estimate of how long the job might take.

Experts' Insight

Tricks of the trade can make all the difference in helping you do a job quickly and well. Experts' Insight gives you useful tips on how to make the job easier.

TOOLS TO USE

The right tools can make a job easier. If a tool or jig will help you with a project, this box will tell you about it and how to use it.

CAUTION!

When a how-to step requires special care, Caution! warns you what to watch out for. It will help keep you from doing damage to yourself or the job at hand.

MEASUREMENTS

Precise measuring and marking are crucial to woodworking success. This box will show standard dimensions and tips for making accurate measurements.

Chapter One

Storage and Shelving

Shelving can be strictly functional, such as open-shelf units in a garage or basement built to hold everything from garden tools to off-season holiday decorations. Or a shelf can be purely decorative, providing a place to display treasured objects. In many cases, shelving and storage units must meet both requirements; they must be spacious and sturdy yet attractive enough to fit into living spaces. Bookcases and entertainment centers are some of the storage units that must be functional as well as good-looking.

Whatever kind of shelving or storage you need in your home, you can often save money by building your own. And you can build each unit to fit your needs exactly.

PLANNING FOR STORAGE

Before you build storage and shelving units, decide what you need. Consider the size and weight of items you need to put on shelves or in cabinets. Plan shelves so they will be deep enough and far enough apart to hold the items. Design garage or basement storage shelves so you can put bulky or heavy items on the lowest shelves for ease of handling.

Bookcases, entertainment centers, or other shelving and storage units in living areas can be freestanding units or built-ins. Built-in storage should match the architectural style of the room as much as possible. Freestanding units often look best if they are similar in style to other furniture in the room.

Storage and shelving ideas

Closet cleanup

Closets can almost always benefit from better organization. You can buy commercial closet organizers or build your own. See pages 68–69 for more about closets.

Cozy corner

A corner of an attic becomes a cozy spot for sitting and reading with a built-in bench and bookshelves. The square openings become a design element. Pages 72–73 show one way to build a bench and bookcases.

Stairway storage

Open shelves under basement stairs (right) create storage in otherwise unusable space. On the main floor of a home, you can still make use of the space, as shown below. See pages 30–33 for ideas about understair shelves and utility shelves.

Crafty closet

This closet has been set up as a hideaway crafts center. Simple shelves hold supplies and baskets with projects in progress. The workbench backboard holds tools and has places for notes and rolls of ribbons to keep the work surface clear.

Retreat with a view

Bookcases and a window seat are perfect together for a den, library, bedroom, sunroom, or any other room where a place to relax would be welcome. Pages 72–73 show how to build a window seat.

High-style shelves

Shelves and cabinets like these are an impressive addition to a room. You could make this type of cabinetry as a built-in or freestanding unit, following the bookcase project on pages 24–25 as a guide.

Out in the open

Open shelves, some hanging from the ceiling and others attached to the wall, provide plenty of storage while maintaining an open, airy feeling in this kitchen. Supports for the wall shelves add to the style. Supports for the suspended shelves, fabricated from pipe and steel rod, are attached solidly to ceiling framing.

Locker room

Keeping sports gear, book bags, boots, and shoes organized in an entry hall is easier with shelves. You could make handy storage like this using fixed-shelf units (pages 18–19) of different sizes.

Installing wall-mounted open shelving

Open shelves are simple to install if you are careful to plumb and level the standards. Attach brackets or standards with screws driven into studs.

Use enough supports so the boards do not sag; see the chart on page 15. If you plan to put very heavy objects on the shelves, add more supports. For a stronger shelf that can span farther, reinforce the front and back edges with a 1×2 attached to the underside of the shelf between the brackets.

You'll Need

TIME: A couple of hours to install a simple set of shelves.
SKILLS: Measuring, leveling, driving screws.
TOOLS: Drill, level, tape measure.

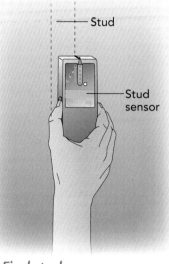

Stud

Stud sensor

1. Find studs.

To find the location of a stud, tap on the wall and listen for a less-hollow sound. Or drill a series of test holes in a place where they will be covered. Better, use a stud sensor.

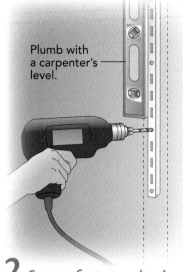

Plumb with a carpenter's level.

2. Secure first standard.

Place a standard over a stud at the desired height. Stamped numerals tell you it is right side up. Drive a screw through the topmost hole at least 1½ inches into a stud. Check for level and drive more screws.

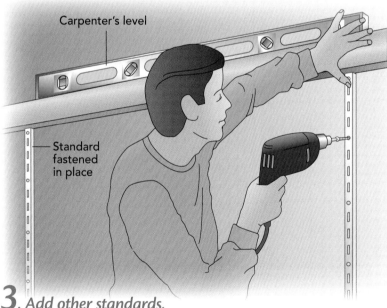

Carpenter's level

Standard fastened in place

3. Add other standards.

Use a level, or a level set on a long straight board, to find the correct height for the standard on the other end of the shelf system. Lightly draw a horizontal line near the intersecting vertical line marking the nearest stud.

Position a standard right side up, with its top edge at the intersection of the two lines. Drive a screw, check for plumb, and drive more screws.

If you will have standards in between the two standards on the ends, use a straightedge set on top of the outside standards to mark for their height. Check them for plumb and attach them with screws.

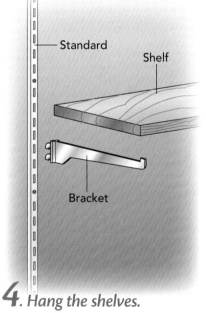

Standard

Shelf

Bracket

4. Hang the shelves.

Use brackets that are the right length for the depth of your shelf. Slip each into two slots and push down until it is secure. Count slots to make sure all the brackets for a shelf are level. When they are installed, simply set the shelf on top. Because the shelves are open-ended, you may need bookends.

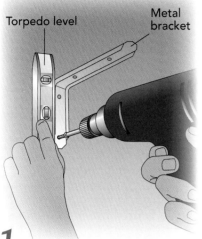

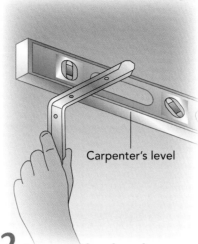

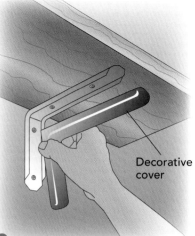

1. Secure the first bracket.

Locate a stud, determine the height of the shelf, and position the bracket. Drive a screw through a hole and into the stud, but do not tighten it completely. Use a level to plumb the bracket (a small torpedo level is handy for this), then drive the other screw and tighten the first screw.

2. Locate other bracket.

Set a level on top of the first bracket and use it to find the height for the bracket near the other end of the shelf. It should be attached to a stud as well. Plumb the bracket and attach it with screws. If there are intermediate brackets, use a straightedge laid on top of the outside brackets to find their height.

3. Attach shelf (and covers).

Lay a shelf on top of the brackets. If the wall is not straight, you may want to trim the shelf so it fits tightly against the wall. Attach the shelf to the brackets by drilling pilot holes and driving ⅝-inch screws up through the bracket. The bracket shown has a decorative cover; simply snap it into place.

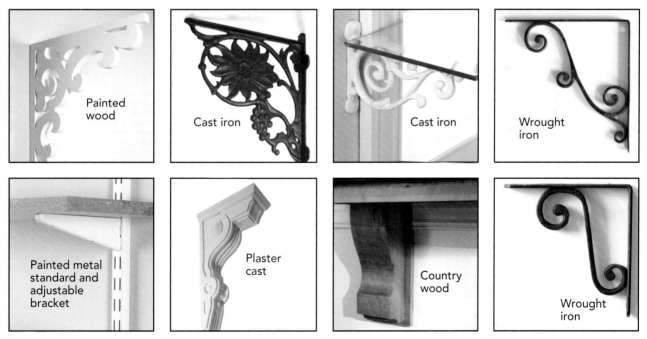

Painted wood

Cast iron

Cast iron

Wrought iron

Painted metal standard and adjustable bracket

Plaster cast

Country wood

Wrought iron

Bracket options.

Choose from a variety of decorative and utility brackets. Diagonal supports lend extra strength but may get in the way of a lower shelf. Choose a bracket nearly as long as the depth of your shelf. For the greatest strength, place the long arm on the wall and the short arm under the shelf.

Brackets are often designed to hide the fasteners; some hook onto screws partially driven into a wood standard so that no hardware is visible.

Using other bracket options

Hardware stores and home centers have a host of options for shelf supports. In addition to the ones shown, consider using coated-wire shelving in places other than a closet (see pages 68–69).

A renovation supply store or an architectural salvage yard will have a variety of interesting old brackets. You may need to strip or paint them, but the results will be well worth your effort.

You can make your own designs and modifications. Design your own wood bracket (see the template below). Trim the shelf with moldings of your choice.

A shelf-support system not only must provide a strong bracket to withstand downward pressure, but it also must ensure that the bracket and shelf do not pull away from the wall. Simply screwing the bracket to the wall may not be sufficient; use a strip attached to the wall, as in the design at right.

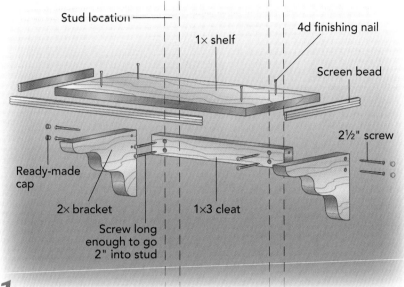

Stud location — 1× shelf — 4d finishing nail — Screen bead — 2½" screw — Ready-made cap — 2× bracket — 1×3 cleat — Screw long enough to go 2" into stud

1. Cut a shelf and add edging.

Cut a piece of ¾-inch plywood or a 1× board to the desired dimensions. For edging choose a ¾-inch-wide screen bead and miter-cut three pieces. Attach the edging using tape and glue (see pages 65 and 120).

Cut a 1×3 cleat to support the back of the shelf and to allow you to attach the brackets anywhere on the wall, since they do not need to be directly screwed into studs. Cut the cleat the length of the shelf, minus the thickness of the brackets and the desired overhangs.

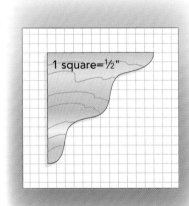

1 square = ½"

2. Design a bracket.

The bracket should be about an inch shorter than the depth of the shelf. Take the design shown above to a copy center and enlarge it until it fits the bracket.

Or draw your own design on graph paper. Use a compass to make a series of connecting arcs. The wider the bracket is in the middle, the stronger it will be.

Jigsaw

3. Cut the bracket.

Cut out the design and trace it onto a piece of 2× lumber. Place it so the bracket's grain will be horizontal when installed.

Clamp the board onto a table corner so that the area under the cut is clear. Cut the line with a jigsaw (see page 97). Use the first bracket as a template for the second bracket. Sand the edges.

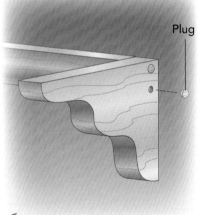

Plug

4. Install the shelf.

Position the cleat level on the wall and mark the location of studs. Drill pilot holes and drive pairs of screws at least 2 inches into each stud. To attach the brackets to the cleat, drill pilot holes and drive two 2½-inch screws. Counterbore and plug the screw holes (see page 103). Attach the shelf to the cleat and brackets with 4d finishing nails.

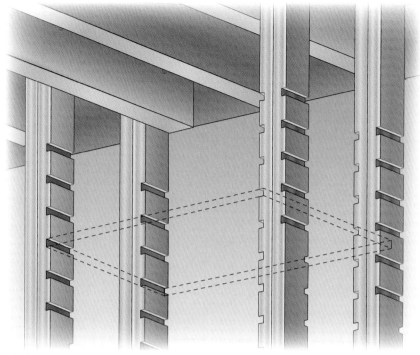

MEASUREMENTS

How many supports do you need?

For shelves that will be loaded with books, space brackets close enough to each other to prevent the shelf from sagging.

Size of Board	Bracket Spacing
¾-inch plywood	32"
1×6 or 1×8	18"
1×10 or 1×12	24"
¾-inch particleboard	18"
2×10 or 2×12	36"
½-inch acrylic	18"
⅜-inch glass	16"

Slide-in utility shelves

This system allows you to move shelves by sliding them out and in again. It produces useful utility shelves but may be too rough-looking for living rooms.

Clamp 2×4 standards, four for each shelf unit, side by side, and cut ¾-inch square dadoes every 2 or 3 inches (see pages 108–111). Strengthen outside standards by screwing them to other 2×4s; screw two dadoed 2×4s together to make inside standards.

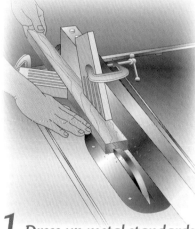

1. Dress up metal standards with hardwood.

Cut a groove the width and depth of the shelf standard into a piece of 1×2 hardwood (see pages 108–111) with a tablesaw or table-mounted router. To groove-cut a piece this narrow with a circular saw, clamp it firmly to a wider 1× piece to provide a flat surface for the saw's baseplate.

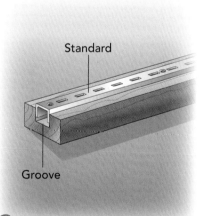

Standard

Groove

2. Install the standard.

Clean out the groove with a chisel. Sand, then apply stain, paint, or a clear finish.

Cut the 1×2 to the exact length of the standard. Slip the standard into the groove. Drill pilot holes for the mounting screws through the hardwood at all the mounting holes.

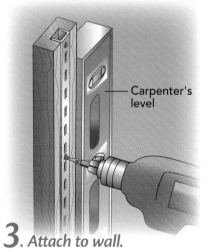

Carpenter's level

3. Attach to wall.

Position the standard over a stud, right side up, at the correct height and use a level to check for plumb (see page 12). Drive screws through the holes in the standard. Choose screws long enough to go at least 1½ inches into the stud. Install the supports and shelves.

Mounting bracketless shelves

Because these shelves have no visible means of support, they seem to float on the wall. They are well supported, however. Lengths of steel reinforcing bar (rebar), used to strengthen concrete, penetrate deep into wall studs and into the shelves.

Determine the spacing precisely—it will be difficult to adjust these shelves later. Once you have drawn level lines on the wall, stand back and make sure they look parallel to the floor. If your floor is obviously out of level, you may want to compensate with the lines. To make the installation easier, use a drill guide so the holes in the shelves and wall are perfectly straight.

You'll Need

TIME: Half a day to lay out and install six shelves.
SKILLS: Careful measuring, leveling, and drilling.
TOOLS: Drill with guide, level, tape measure, saw, hacksaw.

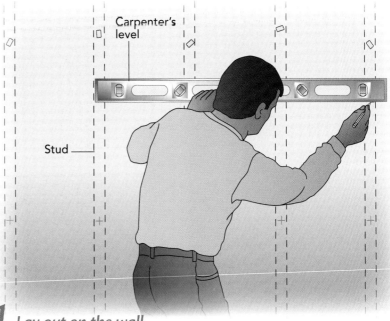

1. Lay out on the wall.

On graph paper diagram the shelves. Choose either a regular pattern or random placement.

Use a stud sensor to locate studs; mark with pieces of tape that can be pulled off without marring the wall. Use a level to draw horizontal lines indicating the centers of the shelves' edges.

Now find the exact center of the studs by drilling exploratory holes or driving a nail at several points. (Make sure that these holes will be covered by the shelf.) At every stud draw an X to indicate the center of the shelf and the center of the stud.

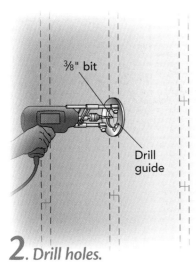

2. Drill holes.

At each X drill a starter hole with an awl or a nail so the drill bit cannot skate away. Using a drill guide to ensure that the holes will be level and straight, drill ⅜-inch holes 3¼ inches deep to accept the rebar.

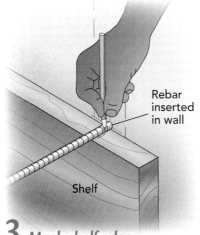

3. Mark shelf edge.

Cut pieces of rebar to the depth of the shelf plus 1 inch, using a hacksaw. Tap a piece of rebar into each hole. With a helper hold the shelf flat against the wall, underneath the rebar pieces. Mark the location of each piece of rebar on the shelf edge.

4. Install shelf.

Use the drill with a guide to bore ⅜-inch holes in the center of the shelf edge for each piece of rebar. Drill carefully and make the holes an inch or so shallower than the board depth. Fit the rods into the holes and tap the shelf flush against the wall.

Other shelf mounting options

Anything that supports a board and keeps it level and perpendicular to a wall is a shelf support. When using flexible materials such as cable or rope as shelf supports, the challenge is to get the spacing between shelves even. (It's difficult to space knots in a rope evenly.) Chain links are easier. You can fine-tune cable brackets by loosening a setscrew.

When hanging a suspended shelf unit, be sure the hook or bracket is strong enough. And always attach it to a framing member (for example, a stud), not just to the wall material.

Sometimes a specialty shelf can be used for other purposes. In the kitchen department of a home center you'll find a number of small shelves designed for the back of cabinet doors; these may be suitable for a workshop or a child's room.

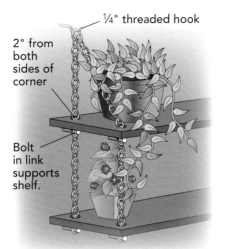

Chains and bolts

Buy chain with links at least 1 inch long and bolts that fit snugly into the links. Drill holes 2 inches in from each shelf edge. Fasten the threaded hooks into studs so each hook is 2 inches from the wall. Insert bolts into links to support the shelves.

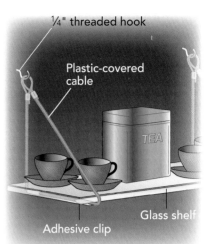

Coated cable and glass

Plastic-covered cables make a stylish support for a glass shelf. Cable crimps form the loops that attach to a threaded hook. Adhesive clips on the cable or cleats on the wall hold the shelf horizontal. You can have glass cut to size and the edges smoothed at a glass shop.

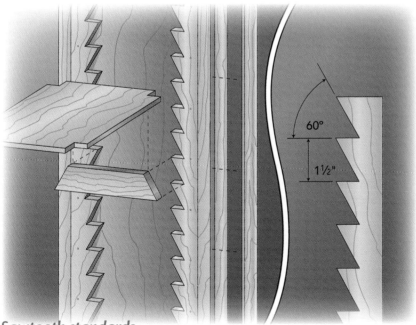

Sawtooth standards

This traditional support system will take time and much cutting. Make standards by cutting thirty 60-degree triangles in 1×2s as shown. A professional-quality jigsaw will help. Make four standards and attach two to each sidepiece. Cut two movable cleats for each shelf. Notch the corners of each shelf so it fits between the standards. Install a plywood back for the unit and attach a fixed shelf near the middle for rigidity.

Experts' Insight
Glass shelves

Sleek and transparent glass shelves ease the difficulty of lighting knickknacks and collections. Here are some installation tips:

■ Have a glass company cut pieces of extra-strength plate glass. Automobile-type safety glass has a plastic layer laminated in the center to prevent splintering and add strength. The edges must be sanded so they are not sharp; you can pay extra and have the corners rounded.

■ Supports for glass should have a soft surface. Glue strips of felt wherever the glass will rest on a hard support.

Building a fixed-shelf unit

Whether you need a freestanding or wall-mounted shelf, a basic box with fixed shelves is sturdy and can be adapted to most any style. Freestanding units can be stacked and moved into new and different configurations; several wall-mounted units can be combined for ease of installation.

Beginner carpenters can make this unit. Butt-joining the outside corners produces a clean-looking joint with little trouble. If you have some carpentry experience, you may want the cleaner look of mitered joints. Try mitered joints only if you are sure of your ability to make perfectly straight miter cuts; gaps will ruin the project.

Simple butt joints are a strong and stable way to attach shelves if fastened with screws. Or reinforce a butt joint by attaching a cleat to the side under the shelf.

A dado joint is strong and virtually guarantees that the shelves and the outside pieces will not warp. When you get the hang of dadoes, cutting them is not time-consuming.

The shelves are simple and require precise cutting. Before starting test your power saw with scrap pieces to make sure you can cut perfectly straight and square without raising splinters. Use a sharp blade. Often it is possible to stack pieces roughly cut to length and make the final cuts on several shelves at once.

The miter-jointed box shown in the steps on page 19 is the most difficult method but hides the end grain so the shelf looks better.

You'll Need

TIME: Most of a day to build a fixed unit with several shelves and a back.
SKILLS: Accurate measuring and cutting, drilling and driving screws, cutting dadoes.
TOOLS: Circular saw, drill, hammer, tape measure, chisel.

Experts' Insight

Finishing or painting a shelf unit

■ Painting a cabinet can be very time-consuming, especially if you need to brush on two coats. Painting boards before they are put together is much easier and faster. Apply a primer coat before assembly. (Many primers dry in an hour or less.) If you want two coats of paint over the primer, apply one coat before assembly.
■ If you need to paint a number of units, consider buying an inexpensive paint sprayer or renting an airless sprayer.
■ Staining assembled shelves is difficult; it's hard to get a consistent color in the corners. Stain the pieces before you assemble them, then apply the clear finish after assembly.

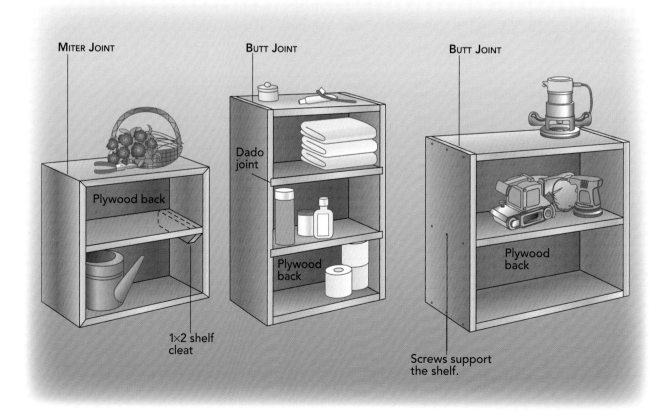

MITER JOINT
Plywood back
1×2 shelf cleat

BUTT JOINT
Dado joint
Plywood back

BUTT JOINT
Plywood back
Screws support the shelf.

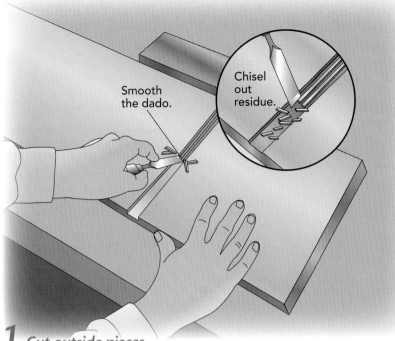

1. Cut outside pieces.

For precise miter cuts rough-cut the outside pieces slightly longer than needed, then cut the miters. Place the two verticals side by side and clamp them firmly. Draw dado layout lines for each shelf and use a scrap piece of shelf to make sure you have marked the width correctly. Cut the dadoes $\frac{5}{16}$ inch deep using a circular saw, radial-arm saw, or tablesaw (see pages 108–111). Clean out the dadoes by chiseling out the waste (see inset). Then use the chisel to smooth the bottom of the groove.

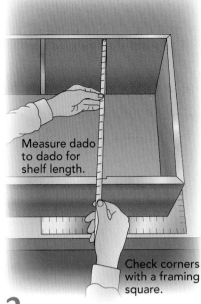

2. Assemble and measure.

Join the pieces into a rectangle by drilling pilot holes and driving $2\frac{1}{4}$-inch finish screws. Check for square as you work. Measure from dado to dado for the lengths of the shelves before cutting the shelves to ensure the best fit.

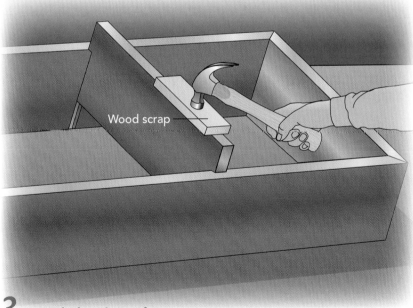

3. Tap shelves into place.

Carefully slip a shelf into both dadoes. Tap it down using a scrap of wood to keep from marring the shelf edge. Avoid tapping one end down farther than the other; alternate between ends every inch or so or gently tap the middle of the shelf to work it into place. When the shelf edges are flush with the edges of the outside pieces, drill pilot holes and drive screws to reinforce and tighten the joints.

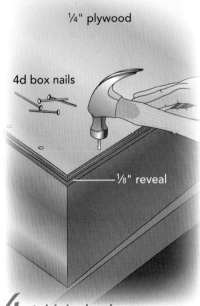

4. Add the back.

Cut a piece of $\frac{1}{4}$-inch plywood $\frac{1}{4}$ inch smaller than the shelf unit in both directions. Center it on the back so there is a $\frac{1}{8}$-inch reveal all around. Drive 4d box nails every 6 inches or so.

Installing adjustable shelves

Inside a frame, support adjustable shelves near each corner and in the middle of the span if needed. The most common method is to use metal support strips with clips, sometimes called pilasters. Attach them to the inside faces of the sidepieces, or cut grooves and set them in (see page 15). You can also opt for one of the pin methods shown on the opposite page.

The important thing is to get all four supports level with each other. Work systematically and double-check often—it's easy to misalign the supports.

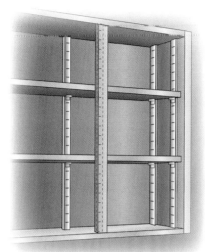

The total system.

Space clips as you would other supports (see the chart on page 15). If the span between vertical outside pieces is too great, install a center stile with a support strip attached. The shelf must be wide enough to fit snugly between the stile and the rear support strip.

Experts' Insight

Tall units need a fixed shelf

■ Place support strips on sidepieces that are stable and strong; if the sides warp, the clips may no longer support the shelf. Support strips will add some rigidity, but not much.
■ If the vertical pieces are made of 1× lumber and are longer than 4 feet, install one fixed shelf about halfway up to ensure that the sides do not bow outward. Attach the shelf with a butt joint or a dado joint (pages 18–19). Then install support strips or pins above and below the fixed shelf.

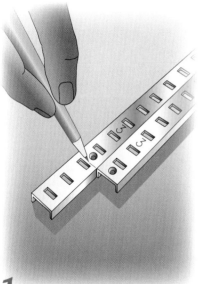

1. Mark for cutting strips.

Cut one piece to the desired height. It doesn't need to extend to the top of the unit, just a notch or two above the top shelf. Use the first piece to measure the others. Line up the slots. To help position the clips later, line up the numbers as well.

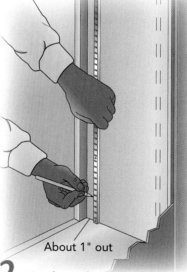

About 1" out

2. Mark and cut grooves.

Position each strip an inch or so from the edge of the unit and trace lines. See pages 108–111 for instructions on cutting grooves. (If you want to set the support strips into grooves, remember to cut the grooves before beginning to assemble the shelf unit.)

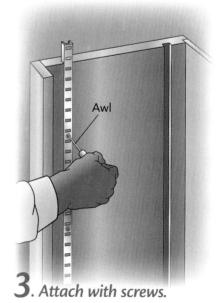

Awl

3. Attach with screws.

Position the support strip and use an awl or sharp pencil to mark for the screws. Drill pilot holes with a drill bit and a depth guide so you won't drill through. A piece of tape wrapped around the drill bit will serve this purpose. Drive screws to attach the support strip.

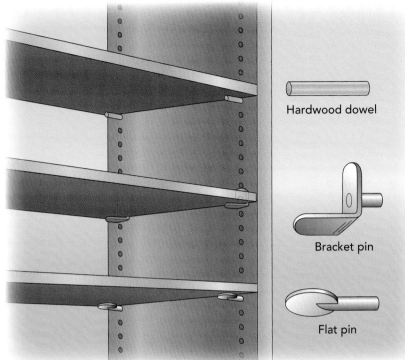

Hardwood dowel

Bracket pin

Flat pin

MEASUREMENTS

Tips for drilling pin holes

■ If the shelf unit has one or more vertical dividers in the middle of the unit, avoid placing holes directly opposite each other on the divider, or else the holes will meet and poke all the way through. To prevent this, offset the vertical lines by ½ inch or so.

■ Save yourself time by drilling only as many holes as you really need. Start at the lowest possible position for the bottom shelf, and end at the highest position for the top shelf.

Pin options

For an inconspicuous support system, drill holes at regular intervals and insert pins. Metal (or plastic) pins come in two types, a flat pin and a bracket pin. Or cut lengths of hardwood dowel to fit into the holes. When using pins, the shelves must fit tightly; if there is more than a ⅛-inch gap between a shelf and the vertical board, the pin could work itself loose and cause the shelf to fall.

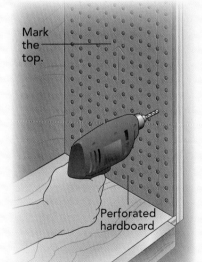

Mark the top.

Perforated hardboard

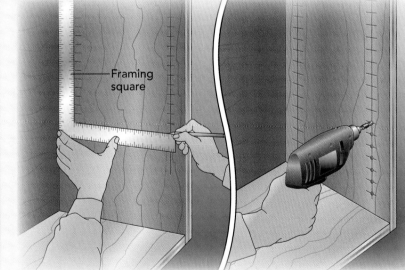

Framing square

Space holes with perforated hardboard ...

Cut a piece of perforated hardboard to fit into the space as a guide. Mark the top end so you always align it the same way.

or use a square.

Draw vertical lines about an inch in from the front and rear edges of the unit. Measure with a framing square or tape measure and mark evenly spaced horizontal lines at one of the vertical lines. Then use a square to copy the horizontal measurements onto the other vertical line. Use a drill bit depth guide so you don't drill through the standard.

Making shelves of found objects

These ideas hark back to the creative shelving solutions found in dorm rooms and first apartments—still classics for informal living areas. If a low-budget, quick shelf suits your plans for a basement family room, a home office, or a hobby room, consider these options. If you have children in your household, limit stacked shelves to less than 3 feet—any higher and they might topple if climbed on. Let these designs spur your imagination to put other found objects to use.

You'll Need

TIME: Gathering the materials will take the most time.
SKILLS: Sawing.
TOOLS: Drill, jigsaw, or handsaw, depending on the project.

Wine crates

These often can be purchased for a few dollars each at a wine store; sometimes they are given away. Stack the crates randomly. Lay one horizontally for tall books. Use one vertically, with a ⅜-inch piece of plywood nailed across the middle to form two shelves for shorter books. For stability, anchor some of the boxes to the wall by driving screws into studs.

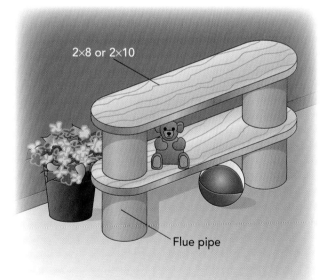

Chimney flue pipes and board

Purchase round clay flue pipe for the vertical supports. Cut the ends of 2×8s or 2×10s in half-circles with a jigsaw to mirror the curve of the pipes. Sand the rough edges. Stain or paint the shelves; the flue pipe is porous enough to take stain, but test it on a scrap piece of pipe first.

Books and boards

Old encyclopedias fastened together make serviceable shelf supports. Clamp each stack and bore two ¼-inch holes down through it. Countersink the holes with a ½-inch bit and slip in a threaded rod cut slightly shorter than the stack is high. Attach washers and nuts and seal the stacks with clear polyurethane.

Making shelves for children

Flexibility and durability are the key for children's shelving and storage structures.

Kids grow fast; a shelving system that can adjust in height and function gives the longest service. When possible make units that can be easily changed, such as the shelf boxes at right. This way children can make it their own by rearranging it to suit their needs.

Pine 1× boards are ideal for these shelves. Give the shelves a coat of durable enamel paint, or stain and finish them to guard against the inevitable marring.

You'll Need

TIME: Several hours for a few boxes; a day for the sports unit.
SKILLS: Measuring and cutting, making dado joints.
TOOLS: Drill, circular saw, hammer, tape measure, square.

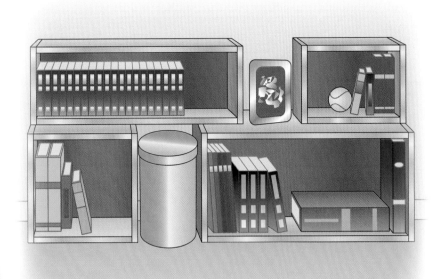

Modular shelving

Make a variety of sizes—different widths, heights, and depths. The spaces between boxes also can be used for storage, so it is not necessary to plan a system precisely. Construct a box with simple butt joints, then reinforce the corners with 3-inch angle brackets. Cut a piece of ¼-inch plywood for the back and use it to help square up the box.

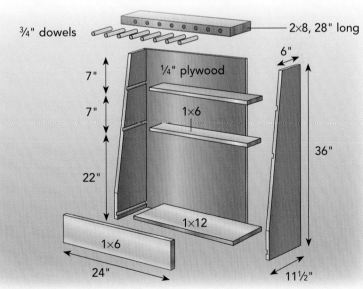

Sports organizer

This keeps sports equipment from cluttering a room. The pegs are handy for hanging gloves, hats, and baseball bats. Large balls go in the lower bin.

Cut and assemble.

Cut sidepieces as shown and cut 5/16-inch-deep dadoes (pages 108–111) for the shelves. Cut the shelves and fasten them in the dadoes with 1⅝-inch trim-head screws. Attach the plywood back with 4d box nails. Use a guide to drill ¾-inch holes, 3 inches deep, into the 2×8; insert the dowels. Attach the 2×8 so it overhangs evenly on both sides.

Building a classic shelf unit

This handsome unit looks elaborate yet does not call for extraordinary skills or tools. The shelves are designed for strength: Reinforced with 1×2s on edge, the shelves can span 4 feet even when loaded with a full set of encyclopedias. Use birch plywood to make the sides and the shelves, and pine moldings if you want to paint the unit. If you choose to stain it, use hardwood 1×10 for the shelves. Select decorative trim along the top and bottom to suit your decor.

You'll Need

TIME: 1½ days.
SKILLS: Cutting moldings, drilling support holes, fastening with nails and screws.
TOOLS: Drill, square, miter box, tape measure, hammer, circular saw, jigsaw.

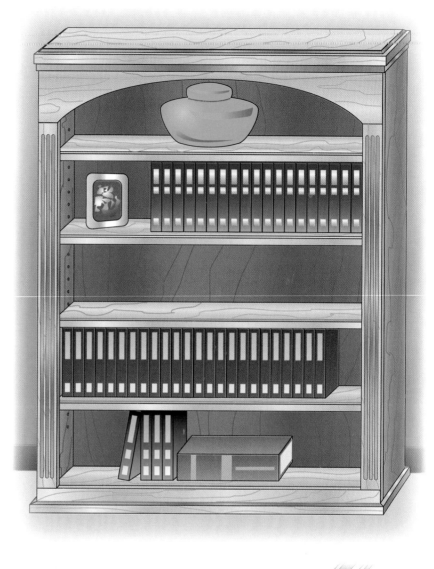

1. Prepare for construction.

The laminated case sides are very rigid, so they won't bow out under the pressure of long shelves full of books. To make them, rip-cut pieces of plywood to 11⅛ inches, or use 1×12s. Cut them to the height of the unit, or cut them a little short and install moldings that increase the height an inch or so.

If the unit will run all the way to the ceiling, attach 1×2 nailers on the ceiling; you'll attach the case sides to these. You can then install crown molding or cove molding at the joint between the shelf and the ceiling.

If the unit will not reach to the ceiling, consider installing a piece of plywood or 1× lumber fitted into the space between the case sides, the top facepiece, and the wall.

Attach a piece of ½-inch plywood to the back of the unit, or attach the case sides directly to the wall.

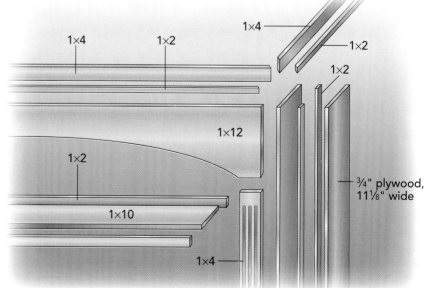

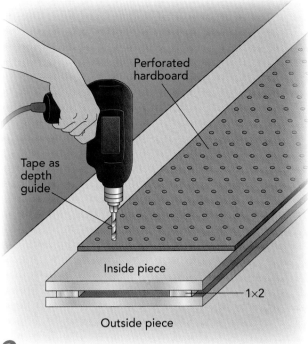

2. Make the case sides.

Lay the outside piece of each case side on a flat surface. Position the 1×2s on them, then the inside piece. Drill pilot holes, using a depth guide so you don't drill through, and drive 2-inch trim-head screws spaced about 4 inches apart. Drill holes for bracket pins using perforated hardboard as a template (see page 21).

3. Build the face.

Cut the top, bottom, and two sides for the face. Draw a long curve along the bottom edge of the top piece, beginning and ending 3½ inches from each end. Cut with a jigsaw (see page 97). Working on a large, flat surface, join the sidepieces to the top and bottom with blind dowels (see page 106).

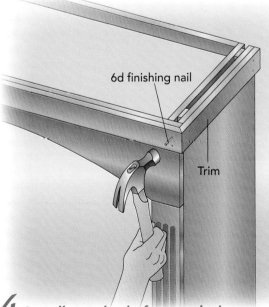

4. Install standards, face, and trim.

Have a helper hold the case sides upright while you attach the face. The outside edges of the face should be flush with the outside faces of the case sides. Drill pilot holes and drive 1⅝-inch trim-head screws every 6 inches. Attach a backpiece and anchor the back to the wall, or anchor the case sides to the wall with angle brackets. Install trim above and below.

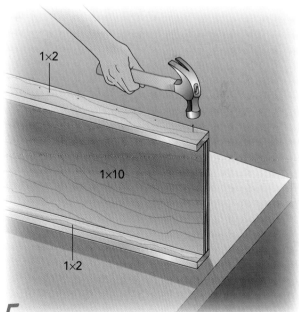

5. Make shelves.

Measure the distance between the case sides and cut 9½-inch-wide pieces of plywood or 1×10 for shelves. For each shelf, cut two 1×2 edging pieces as long as the shelf. Attach them to the front and back edges of the shelf with white glue and 6d finishing nails. Insert shelving pins into the holes in the standards and place the shelves in position.

Building a plate shelf

This wall-hung plate shelf is an attractive display piece for a kitchen or eating area. Rout grooves or add a front lip on the shelves to safely hold the plates; 1×1 rails in back add a decorative touch and keep the plates from rubbing against the wall. Pegs along the bottom display a collection of mugs.

Pine is a pleasing choice for this informal piece. Stain or a clear finish suits an informal decor; use gloss enamel for easy cleaning if you choose to paint it.

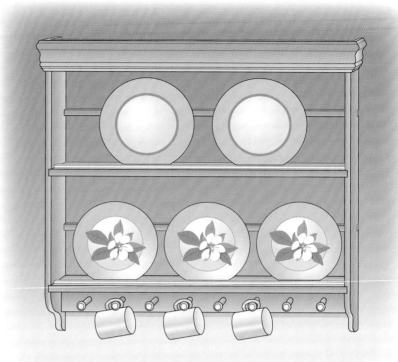

You'll Need

TIME: Most of a day.
SKILLS: Measuring and cutting, making dado joints, miter-cutting molding, drilling.
TOOLS: Circular saw or tablesaw, drill, square, tape measure.

Cut pieces and assemble.

Cut the two sidepieces to length. Make a template for the bottom curved cut similar to the one shown on page 14 and cut it with a jigsaw. Cut 5/16-inch-deep rabbets at the top and dadoes for the shelves (see pages 108–111). Cut 3/4-inch-square notches in the back of each sidepiece for the two rails.

Cut and join the shelves by gluing, drilling pilot holes, and driving 6d nails. Cut the rails to length and attach with glue and nails. (If 1×1 is not available, rip-cut a piece of 1× lumber to 3/4 inch.) Cut the 1×3 cup rack to fit between the sidepieces. Use a drill with a guide to bore regularly spaced 3/4-inch holes that angle slightly upward. Buy Shaker pegs or cut pieces of 3/4-inch dowel to 3 inches and sand the edges. Squeeze some white glue into each hole and tap in the pegs. Attach the cup rack with 6d finishing nails driven from the sides. Miter and install the trim.

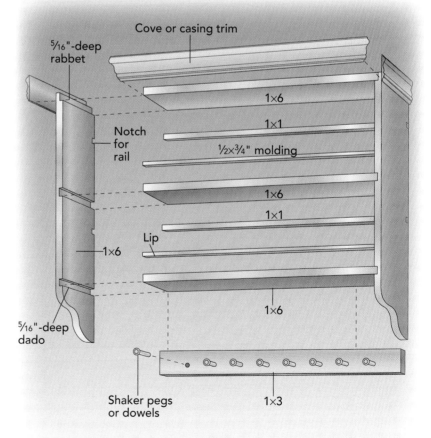

Cove or casing trim

5/16"-deep rabbet

Notch for rail

1×6

1×1

1/2×3/4" molding

1×6

1×1

Lip

1×6

1×6

5/16"-deep dado

1×6

Shaker pegs or dowels

1×3

Installing an arched niche

Making this charming alcove for a flower vase or piece of sculpture is not so much building a shelf as reshaping the wall.

Most wall studs are placed 16 inches on center, making a space of 14½ inches between them for the niche. If studs are closer together (as they may be near the end of a wall), you can make a narrower niche. If electrical or plumbing lines run through the space, you will have to do this project somewhere else.

You'll Need

TIME: 1 day, plus time for three coats of joint compound to dry.
SKILLS: Cutting, gluing and clamping, patching a wall.
TOOLS: Hammer, crosscut saw, keyhole saw, clamps, wallboard taping knives.

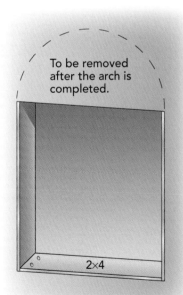

1. Cut the hole.

Locate the wall studs. Drill a small hole and insert an unbent coat hanger to test whether there is enough space or if there is wiring or plumbing behind the space. If there isn't, use a keyhole saw to cut out a rectangle from stud to stud. Install a level 2×4 at the bottom of the hole, toenailing it to the studs.

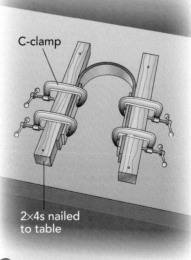

2. Make the arch.

Nail two 2×4s to a piece of plywood, spaced as far apart as the opening. Cut six long strips of mat board the depth of the wall. Laminate them with carpenter's glue and shape them into an arch. Clamp the sides to the 2×4s and allow the arch to dry. Cut the mat-board arch to the proper height.

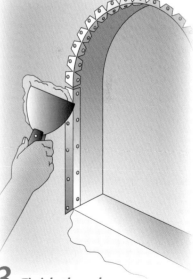

3. Finish the edge.

Use the arch as a template to mark the wall and cut it out. Insert the arch, then glue it to the studs with construction adhesive. Attach flexible corner bead to the outside edge and drywall tape to the inside edges. Apply several coats of joint compound, sand smooth, and paint to match the wall.

Installing recessed shelving

Recessed shelves are great spacesavers, ideal for collectibles and knickknacks. Setting shelves inside a wall looks more difficult than it actually is; checking that the wall cavity is free of electrical and plumbing lines and cutting a clean opening are the most difficult steps. Otherwise you simply build a fixed-shelf unit (see pages 18–19) and insert it in the wall. The unit shown here spans two studs. If a unit that's 14½ inches wide will suit your needs, you can build it without cutting a stud.

You'll Need

TIME: A full day.
SKILLS: Cutting walls, basic cabinetmaking.
TOOLS: Jigsaw or keyhole saw, reciprocating saw, drill, hammer, tape measure, level.

Stud

Jigsaw

CAUTION!
Is it a load-bearing wall?

Some interior walls are simply partitions between rooms. Others are load-bearing walls that support the roof or a wall on the floor above. Walls that run parallel to joists above are not usually load-bearing. Outside walls are load-bearing, and walls that run perpendicular to overhead joists may be load-bearing as well. Check by taking measurements to see whether a wall above is directly on top of the wall you want to cut into. Do not cut a stud in a load-bearing wall. Consult with a carpenter if you are not sure.

1. Lay out and cut the wall.

Locate studs by rapping on the wall, drilling test holes, or using a stud sensor. Drill holes and insert an unbent coat hanger to explore the wall bay. Do not cut the wall if electrical or plumbing lines are between the studs.

Cut the drywall with a jigsaw or keyhole saw. (If the wall is plaster, cutting will be difficult: Score lines deeply with a knife first to prevent cracking the surrounding area.) Cut alongside the studs for vertical lines; mark horizontal cut lines with a level.

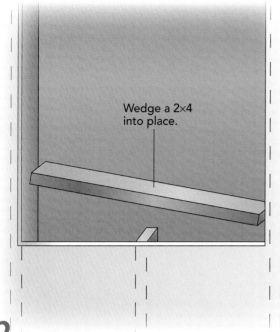

Wedge a 2×4 into place.

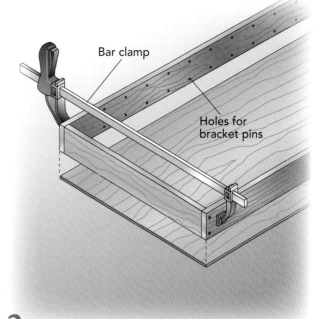

Bar clamp

Holes for bracket pins

2. Cut the stud and put in a sill and header.

Cut the center stud at the bottom and top with a reciprocating saw. Or cut as deeply as you can with a circular saw, then finish the cut with a handsaw. Do not cut through the wall surface on the other side. Cut a 2×4 sill for the bottom and a header for the top to fit the opening. Level them and attach them with screws.

3. Build the recessed unit.

Build a shelf unit like this butt-joined frame with adjustable shelves resting on support pins (see pages 20–21). Rip-cut the boards to the depth of the opening, less ¼ inch for the backpiece. Make the unit ½ inch smaller than the opening on all sides. Before assembling, drill holes for bracket pins.

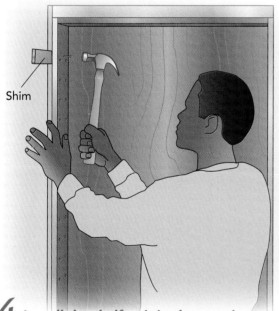

Shim

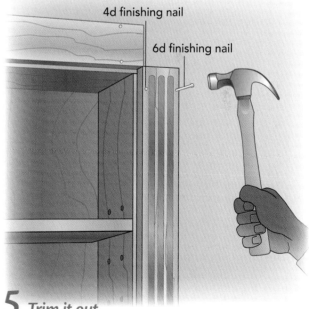

4d finishing nail

6d finishing nail

4. Install the shelf unit in the opening.

Set the unit in place. Check for level and plumb and make sure the front edge is flush with the wall surface. Use shims if necessary. Drill pilot holes and drive 6d finishing nails through the sides, top, and bottom.

5. Trim it out.

Install molding around the perimeter. Butt-joined casing is the simplest, although you may prefer to miter the corners or use corner blocks. Drill pilot holes to avoid splitting the wood and drive 6d nails into studs and 4d nails into the shelf unit.

Adding understair shelves

The area under a basement stairway often goes to waste; stacking boxes there is awkward because the space is triangular. A shelf system provides a convenient place to store canned goods, bulk purchases, and sports equipment.

Because basement floors may become damp, the bottom shelf should be elevated on pressure-treated 2×4 sleepers, which will not rot even if they get wet occasionally.

Rather than measuring each upright individually—a complicated process—the technique shown here allows you to quickly cut the outline of the triangle, then make shelves to fit it.

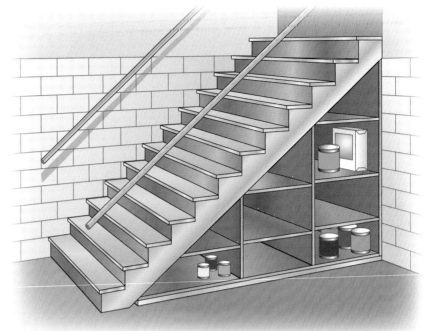

You'll Need

Time: Most of a day.
Skills: Careful measuring, making bevel cuts, fastening with screws.
Tools: Circular saw, drill, T-bevel, level, framing square, chalkline.

Understair shelves

Basic shelves like these can be quickly assembled with screws. Offset the shelves so they do not line up horizontally; that way you will be able to drive screws straight through the uprights and into the shelves. For a more finished look and for greater strength, you can set the shelves in dadoes (see pages 108–111) cut into the uprights.

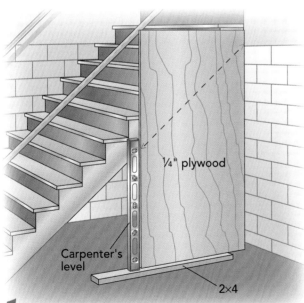

1. Mark and cut backing plywood.

Place a piece of ¼-inch plywood against the stairway, resting it on top of a piece of 2×4, positioned along the stairway where it will be at the back of the shelves. Be sure to check for plumb before measuring and marking. Mark each side, snap a chalkline, and cut. Do the same for the other backing pieces.

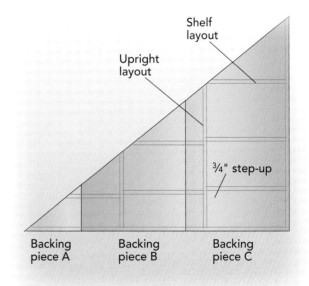

2. Lay out on the backing pieces.

Test to see that the backing pieces fit. Then lay them down and draw layout lines indicating shelves and uprights. Step up each shelf ¾ inch so you can fasten each from the side. Avoid making unusable small triangular shelves. The shelves will be wide; use ¾-inch plywood so they won't sag.

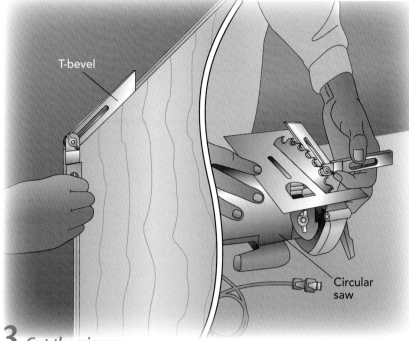

T-bevel

Circular saw

3. Cut the pieces.

Cut the pieces to fit the layout. The uprights and shelves should be bevel-cut where they meet the stringer, as shown in the layout drawing below. To cut the bevels, hold a T-bevel against the plywood backing pieces to find the correct angle, and transfer that angle to a circular saw, tablesaw, or radial-arm saw. Measure the layout lines and cut all the bevels.

Pressure-treated 2×4

4. Attach floor sleepers.

Cut two pieces of pressure-treated 2×4 to fit along the bottom of the shelf system. Attach them to a concrete floor with 2-inch masonry nails every foot or so.

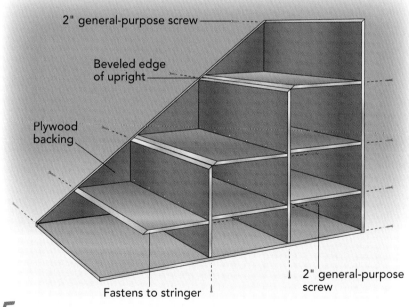

2" general-purpose screw

Beveled edge of upright

Plywood backing

Fastens to stringer

2" general-purpose screw

5. Assemble the shelf unit.

Place the shelves and uprights on the backing pieces to make sure they are correctly cut. Use a framing square to line up the shelves. Attach the components by driving 2-inch general-purpose screws every few inches at each joint. Check for square continually and make sure none of the pieces extends beyond the plywood backing. Slide the assembled unit into place and fasten the beveled shelf edges to the stringer.

Experts' Insight

Building plywood shelves

■ Plywood can soak up a lot of paint, making finishing a costly and time-consuming job. Consider covering the shelf tops with shelf paper and giving the other surfaces a quick coat of polyurethane. If you choose to paint, birch-veneer plywood soaks up less paint than pine.

■ Whenever cutting across the surface grain of plywood, first score the cutline with a utility knife to minimize splintering. You do not need to do this when cutting with the grain.

■ Give exposed plywood edges a quick sanding with a hand sander to remove burrs and to prevent splintering.

Building utility shelves and racks

Utilitarian shelves and racks for a workshop or garage can be made of plywood and 2× lumber. Locate them so lumber and sheet goods can be easily stacked and removed. Make some shelves deep enough for your largest items, and others shallower so cans of paint and the like don't get lost in back. Before you buy lumber to build your own unit, check the storage options at a home center. Ladder brackets (right) and metal shelf units are often more cost-effective than shelves built from scratch.

You'll Need

Time: Half a day or less for any of these projects
Skills: Basic measuring, cutting, and fastening skills.
Tools: Circular saw, drill, square, level, chalkline.

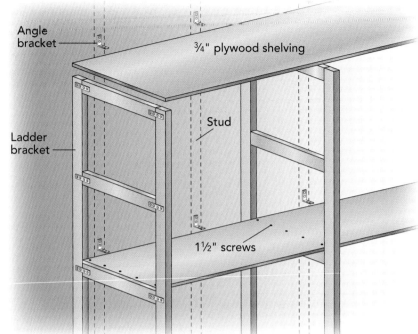

Store-bought ladder brackets

Ready-made ladder brackets are available at most home centers and will probably cost little more than homemade. Have helpers hold the ladder brackets plumb while you attach ¾-inch plywood shelving with screws. Anchor the unit to the wall with angle brackets and screws driven into studs.

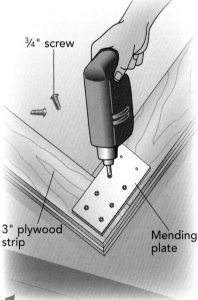

1. Build lumber racks.

Cut 3-inch-wide strips of plywood and assemble them into a U-shape, using mending plates and ¾-inch screws to join them.

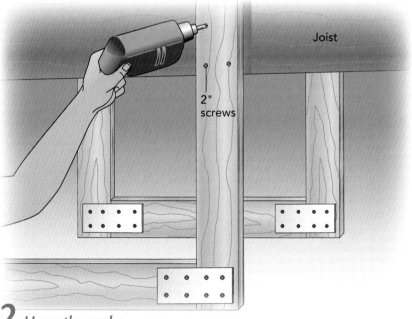

2. Hang the racks.

Chalk a line on the underside of the joists so that the racks will be in line with each other. Attach the tops of the racks to joists by driving four 2-inch screws through each of the plywood supports and into the joists. Stack the lumber neatly, putting the widest pieces on the bottom to support the other boards and to keep them from warping.

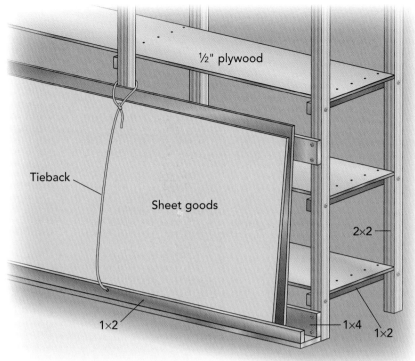

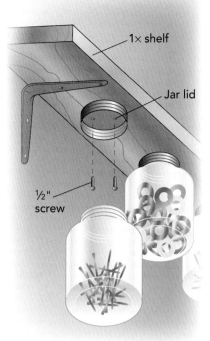

Shelves and plywood storage

This arrangement will keep sheet goods easily accessible and prevent them from warping. Build standard shelves with 2×2 uprights and 1×2 horizontal supports. Make the bottom plywood channel out of two 1×4s and one 1×2; drill pilot holes and drive screws to fasten them into a U-shape. Drill a hole in the middle of the 1×2 and tie a rope to it. Use the rope to hold sheets of plywood securely in place.

Hanging jars.

Your grandfather may have used this system to organize screws and small items, and it still works. Drive screws to fasten jar lids to the underside of a shelf, and screw the jar onto the lid.

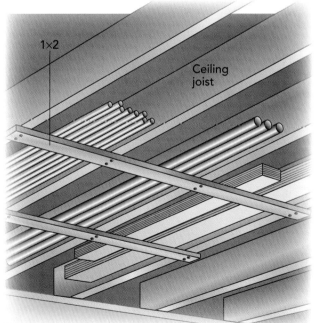

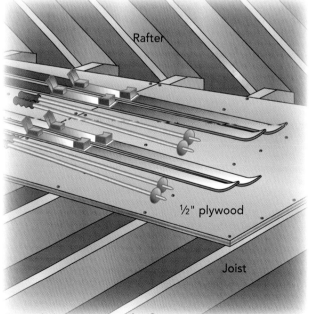

Between-joist storage

Use the space between open joists in a garage or basement to store lumber, pipes, or other long objects. Attach 1×2s to the underside of the joists for an instant rack. If the stored objects will be heavy, attach 2×4s instead of 1×2s.

Over-joist storage platform

If your garage or attic has space above the joists, slide pieces of ½-inch plywood onto them and attach the plywood to the joists with 1¼-inch screws. Make the platform roomy and leave enough empty space on the sides so you can easily get to all the stored objects.

Chapter Two

Kitchen Cabinets

Cabinets often make the difference between a kitchen that's a great place to cook—or even entertain—and one that's barely tolerable to be in. Everything about the cabinetry makes a difference in how you regard your kitchen—the functionality of the cabinets themselves, how they are arranged in the room, and their style and appearance.

Kitchen remodeling is one of the most common home improvement projects. Installing cabinets in a new or remodeled kitchen is a job almost any do-it-yourselfer can accomplish. This chapter shows how to plan a layout for new kitchen cabinets, how to select factory-built units, and how to install them. Installing the cabinets yourself can save a lot of money.

BUILD YOUR OWN

This chapter also has instructions for building your own kitchen cabinets. The construction is fairly simple; it's basically a plywood box with a face frame attached to the front edge.

Building your own allows you to match existing cabinets that you want to retain or to construct a custom island or peninsula. When a stock-size cabinet won't quite fit your kitchen design, you can build exactly what you need.

You can also follow the kitchen cabinet design to build bathroom vanities, built-ins for living rooms, family rooms, and other living spaces, and workshop and hobby room cabinets. You can add cabinet latches to make lockable storage for basements and garages too.

Kitchen cabinet ideas

Crowning touch

A crown molding along the tops of the wall cabinets adds a finishing touch to this installation. The visible cabinet sides are dressed up with raised-panel construction that matches the doors.

Behind the curtain

Open shelves recessed into the wall (see pages 28–29) provide plenty of space and ready access for dishes, serving pieces, and glassware. A curtain screens the shelves.

Going to the top

These tall wall cabinets extend to the ceiling, eliminating the usual space above the cabinets. Painted doors and drawers on some of the stained cabinets match the wall to create a unique style.

Traditional view

Cabinet doors with glass panes give this kitchen an early 20th-century farmhouse look. The glass and white-painted cabinetry make the kitchen seem light and bright. To hide the cupboard contents, you could use frosted or pebbled glass.

Warm wood

Stained and clear-finished wood cabinetry lends a warm look to a kitchen. A high-quality gloss or semigloss polyurethane is durable and easy to keep clean, making it a good clear finish for kitchens.

Household office

This kitchen includes a desk-height work surface that makes a great place to sit down and pay bills or plan menus. Place the office area at the edge of the kitchen so it won't be in the way of cooking.

Colorized cabinets

Imaginative paint gives these standard cabinets a distinctive look. The solid-color face frames set off doors and drawer fronts painted with a multicolor decorative technique. The second and third drawers in the five-drawer base cabinet (right side back) have been replaced with shelves and doors.

Top row

A second tier of cabinets above the standard wall cabinets increases the storage in this kitchen. Frosted glass inserts in the doors add style without showing what's inside.

Island dream

A curved end takes this island beyond the ordinary. The rounded end unit could be built to add on to a standard cabinet, or the entire structure could be custom-built.

Flipper kitchen

Top cabinets in this kitchen have flip-up doors for easy access. A shallow shelf below the cabinets can become display or storage space.

Built-in sideboard

Kitchen cabinets installed in a niche in the wall (a closet with the door and jamb removed could work too) make a handy sideboard in this dining room. For entertaining, the top can be cleared for serving food or beverages.

Room at the top

You don't have to enclose the space above wall cabinets. This open shelving makes a great place to display a collection of cookie jars and pottery.

Laying out kitchen cabinets

Use your present cabinets as a starting place for kitchen planning. Are your pans crammed into one cabinet? Plan to move them near the cooktop and store them in built-in pullout shelves. Can you store all your dishware near the dishwasher? Plan to store items close to where they're used.

Kitchen designers talk about the work triangle—the path between the cooktop, the refrigerator, and the sink and dishwasher. The triangle should be located away from traffic patterns through the kitchen. The total distance around it should be between 12 and 27 feet, so each leg of the work triangle should be from 4 to 9 feet long.

Standard kitchen base cabinets are 34 1/2 inches tall and 22 inches deep, so the countertop will be 36 inches high and 24 inches deep. Wall cabinets are usually 12 inches deep and may be 30, 36, or 42 inches tall. The bottom of a wall cabinet is usually 18 inches above the countertop—54 inches above the floor.

An island can be made from a standard base cabinet: Cover the unfinished sides with plywood that matches the rest of the cabinets.

Refrigerator dimensions affect layout: Side-by-side models can be up to 35 inches wide and 69 inches tall; single-door models are usually 30 to 32 inches wide, up to 67 inches tall. Both leave room for a short wall cabinet above. Or you can install a cabinetlike 27-inch-wide modular refrigerator.

Experts' Insight
Work order

Every cabinet installation is unique, but the major stages should proceed in this order:
■ Demolition and removal of existing cabinets; rough wiring, plumbing, and ductwork.
■ Patching and priming walls; installing flooring.
■ Installing cabinets; finish painting; countertops.
■ Finish plumbing and electrical—sink, dishwasher, cooktop, oven, range hood.

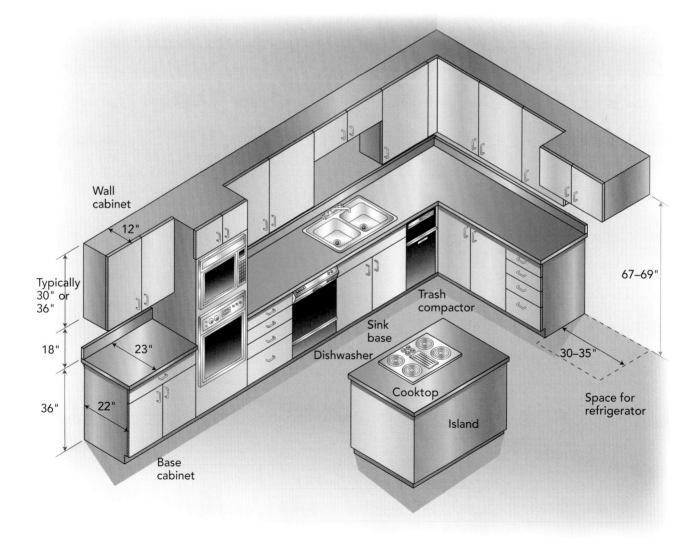

Wall cabinet — 12" — Typically 30" or 36" — 18" — 23" — 36" — 22" — Base cabinet — Dishwasher — Sink base — Cooktop — Island — Trash compactor — 67–69" — 30–35" — Space for refrigerator

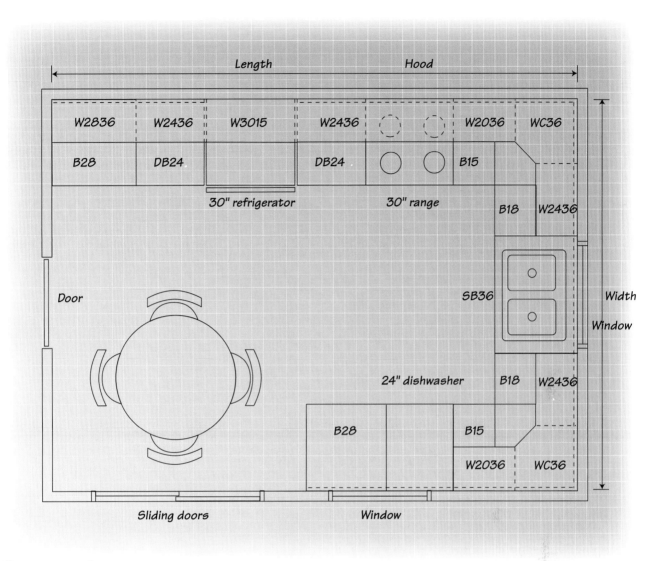

Length Hood

W2836 W2436 W3015 W2436 W2036 WC36

B28 DB24 DB24 B15

30" refrigerator 30" range

B18 W2436

Door SB36 Width

Window

24" dishwasher B18 W2436

B28 B15

W2036 WC36

Sliding doors Window

Draw up a plan

Begin by making your own plan with graph paper, tracing paper, pencil, and a straightedge. Make the drawing to scale—for instance, have each graph paper square equal 4 inches. Measure your kitchen carefully. Check to see that walls are plumb and square; if not, you may have an inch less space than you think. Draw the basic floor plan on graph paper, then overlay tracing paper to try out different cabinet layouts.

Some cabinet retailers have computer programs to help design your project. The programs even show you what the cabinets will look like from various angles—and what the cabinets will cost. If you have access to a design computer, your plan will provide essential dimensions and give you a head start on the design.

Use these standard cabinet designations: B (base cabinet), W (wall cabinet), DB (drawer base), WC (corner wall cabinet), CB (corner base cabinet), SB (sink base). Dimensions (in inches) come after these designations. The first number refers to width, and the second refers

to height. All base cabinets are 34½ inches tall, so they have only one number for the width. For example, "DB18" means a drawer base 18 inches wide; "W3036" is a wall cabinet 30 inches wide and 36 inches tall.

Manufactured cabinets come in a limited number of standard sizes, so you will have to choose an ensemble of different sizes that fit the space. You can build your own cabinets (pages 46–52) in any sizes you want.

Place cabinets where they are most convenient. For instance, position a drawer base for silverware near the dishwasher and put a large base cabinet for pots and pans near the range. Do not plan for cabinets to fit tightly, or you may not be able to squeeze them all in. Allow room for a 1- to 3-inch spacer at the end of every run. Leave plenty of room for your range and refrigerator; they should not fit too snugly. Check manufacturers' recommendations for openings.

Plan for furniture as well as cabinets. In the example above, there is just enough room for a table with chairs.

Choosing cabinets

While the decorating style of cabinets can vary widely, there are only a few essential configurations. When considering these configurations, remember that the doors should swing open in directions that allow for easy access. Storage accessories (see pages 56–57) can be added to suit your storage requirements.

Base cabinets have toe spaces 3½ to 4 inches high and 3 inches deep so you can stand next to the countertop comfortably. The most common base cabinet has a single drawer on top and two shelves below. If the cabinet is wider than 24 inches, it will have two drawers and two doors. You may be able to save money by buying a few larger cabinets instead of several smaller cabinets. Most kitchens need at least one drawer base. Make sure that the sink base has enough room for the sink and its plumbing.

Sometimes the layout will call for a shallow base cabinet, to allow for the swing of a back door, for example. Use a 30-inch-tall wall cabinet (which is 12 inches deep). Set it on 1×4s (¾×3½ inches in actual dimension) to mimic the toe space of standard base cabinets and add a 1-inch spacer on top.

Tall wall cabinets provide more storage space for not much more money; but if you can't reach the top shelf, it may not be of much use. Most people prefer 30- or 36-inch-tall wall cabinets, although 40-inch-tall cabinets are available.

Corner cabinets have hard-to-reach spaces; a lazy Susan in either a wall or a base corner cabinet may be the solution.

For maximum storage where you do not need a countertop, install a pantry cabinet.

A spacer for a wall cabinet is simply a piece of 1× lumber stained to match the cabinet. A spacer for a base cabinet includes a toe-kick.

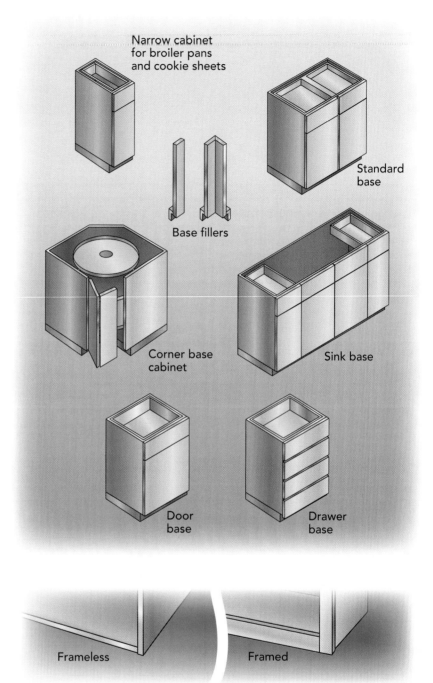

Framed and frameless cabinets

Framed cabinets usually have 1×2 frame pieces to provide rigidity. Frameless cabinets rely on the cabinet walls for strength. Framed cabinets allow for a variety of hinge types; frameless cabinets have Euro-style hinges (see page 116).

Frameless cabinets offer a cleaner look and use space more efficiently. However, you must use spacers in corners so that the doors can open completely.

Framed cabinets offer a more traditional appearance, are stronger overall, and are easier to install. However, both the door and drawer openings are smaller than those in frameless cabinets.

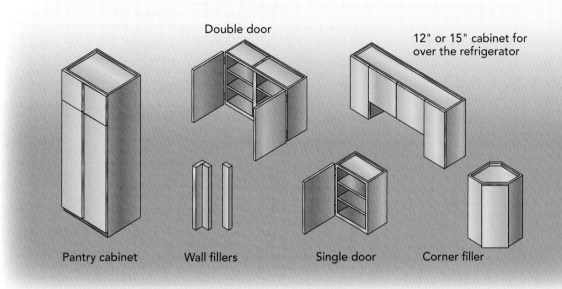

Double door

12" or 15" cabinet for over the refrigerator

Pantry cabinet

Wall fillers

Single door

Corner filler

Purchasing options for kitchen cabinets

If you want to buy kitchen cabinets, choose from the following purchasing strategies.

■ Ready-to-assemble (RTA) and unfinished cabinets are usually the least-expensive option. You can find these stacked on large shelves in home centers. They take some time to assemble and/or finish, but they may be worth the trouble. Be sure you can purchase fillers, wire racks, and other amenities that will fit the brand you choose. Unfinished cabinets offer savings, but be realistic about your ability to achieve a consistent finish.

■ Stock preassembled cabinets range from 9 to 48 inches in width, in 3-inch increments. Most large manufacturers have a catalog that lists cabinet types and amenities. You will have a limited number of finishes and colors to choose from. Watch prices carefully—often the basic cabinets are reasonable,

but prices climb on special cabinet inserts and amenities. Some makers can deliver cabinets within a week.

■ Semi-custom cabinets are built to your exact specifications by the manufacturer. This lets you get cabinets that fit your space exactly, and you can choose your finish. However, style choices may be limited. Also, you'll have to allow weeks or months for delivery. Even less convenient, you'll face a long wait for a replacement if a cabinet is damaged in transit.

■ Custom cabinets are the most expensive. They are measured onsite by the fabricator and made locally, which might mean less wait than with semi-custom cabinets. Also, in most cases, custom cabinets offer the largest selection of finishes and styles to choose from.

Cabinet materials

Take a close look at the cabinets you are considering. Solid wood is usually used for cabinet frames, and sometimes for doors, but rarely for the main body of cabinets. Often cabinets are made of a combination of materials.

■ A word of caution about particleboard: This engineered wood is made by bonding wood fiber with resin. If the material is not well reinforced with solid materials, it will lack strength. Overlong particleboard shelves will sag over time. High-quality particleboard, rated as 45-pound commercial grade, is better than standard; but no particleboard holds fasteners well.

■ Medium-density fiberboard (MDF) has a harder surface than particleboard and will take paint more readily. But it is no stronger than particleboard; hinges should be attached to solid wood frames.

■ Laminates vary in quality. Standard plastic laminates, such as those used on countertops, are strong. Other products, such as melamine, are easily chipped. All laminates are difficult to repair.

■ Plywood, made by laminating thin layers (plies) of wood together, is the best material for structural support. It is very strong, is almost impossible to crack, and takes finishes well.

Building a base cabinet

Professional cabinetmakers make detailed drawings and figure the dimensions for all of the cabinet components before making the first cut. Follow their example: It's the only way to ensure against costly cutting mistakes, and it will save you time in the long run.

Planning cabinet construction requires three steps. First, make scaled drawings of the project on graph paper. Then make a cut list spelling out the exact dimensions of all the parts. Finally, draw a cutting diagram that shows how you will cut out all the pieces.

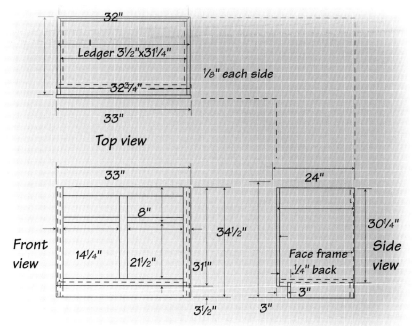

You'll Need

Time: Most cabinets can be built in a day.
Skills: Accurate measuring and cutting, squaring, fastening.
Tools: Circular saw, drill, square, hammer, nail set.

Scaled drawings, cutting diagram

The scaled drawings (above) and the cutting diagram (below) are for a base cabinet 33 inches wide, 24 inches deep, and 34½ inches high. Be sure the plywood grain runs up and down for the sidepieces. You may have to redraw and refigure several times before all of the dimensions come out right.

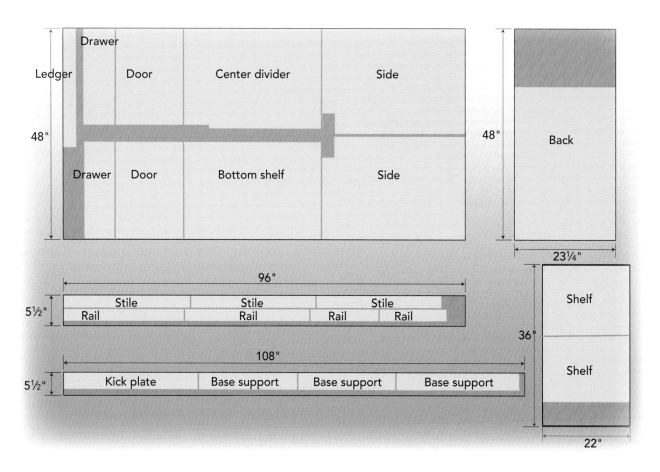

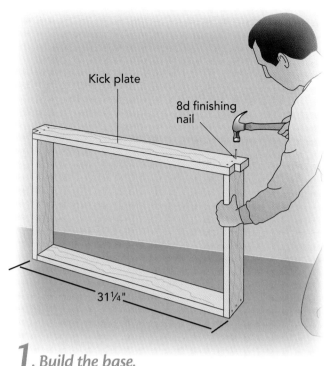

1. Build the base.

Cut the base pieces to size. Working on a flat surface, join the pieces by drilling pilot holes, applying wood glue, and driving three 8d finishing nails at each joint. Check the frame for square as you work. Align the sides with the notched kick plate as shown on the drawing.

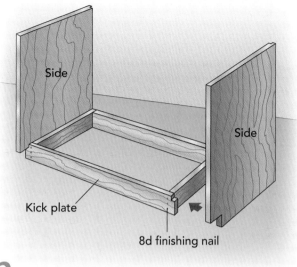

2. Cut and attach the sides.

Cut the cabinet sides, then notch the front edge of each to fit over the notch in the kick plate. Rabbet the back edge of each sidepiece to accommodate the ¼-inch plywood back (see pages 108–111). Drill pilot holes, glue, and drive 8d finishing nails to attach the sides.

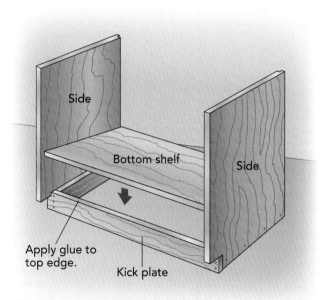

3. Install the bottom shelf.

Cut the bottom shelf to size and test to see that it fits between the sides. Apply glue to the top edge of the base pieces and set the shelf in place. Be sure its front edge is flush with the fronts of the sides. Drill pilot holes and drive 6d finishing nails through the shelf into the base.

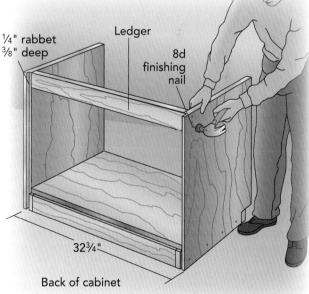

4. Cut and install the ledger.

Double-check the length of the ledger by measuring the distance between the inside edges of the cabinet sides at the bottom of the cabinet. Cutting to this length will ensure that the cabinet is square. Attach the ledger with 8d finishing nails; position it so the backpiece can slip into the rabbet.

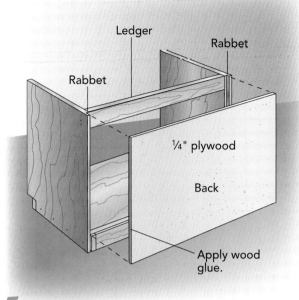

5. Install the plywood back.

Cut a piece of ¼-inch plywood to fit between the rabbets. Take care to cut it perfectly square. It does not need to extend down to the floor, but it must cover the entire back opening. Test the fit and check that the cabinet is square. Drive several 4d finishing nails partway through it near the edges. Lay a bead of wood glue in the rabbet on both sides and fasten with nails driven every few inches.

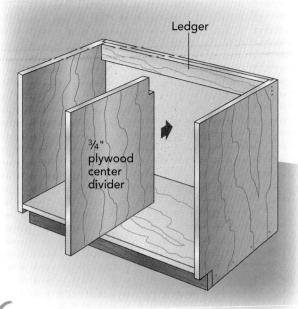

6. Fit in the center divider.

Cabinets wider than 24 inches need two doors and two drawers, so there must be a center divider. Cut a piece of ¾-inch plywood so its front aligns with the front edge of the bottom and its top edge aligns with the top. Make a notch to accommodate the ledger. Position the divider in the center of the cabinet and attach with 8d finishing nails and wood glue.

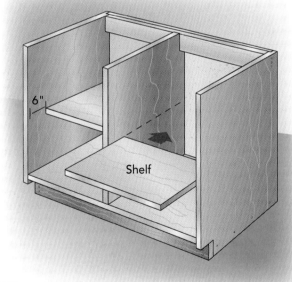

7. Add the shelves.

A base cabinet shelf is usually 6 inches or so shallower than the bottom so that you can reach the pots and pans in the bottom compartment. Cut shelves to fit. Use a framing square to mark the location of the shelves and attach them with wood glue and 8d finishing nails.

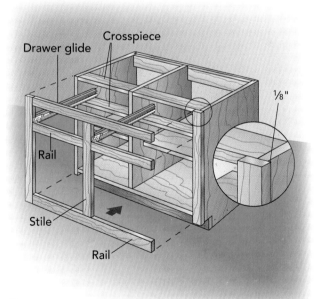

8. Add the face frame and front crosspieces.

Cut four plywood front crosspieces and attach them with glue and 8d finishing nails. Cut the vertical stiles from ¾×1½-inch stock and install them with nails and glue, positioning the outer ones so they extend ⅛ inch past each side of the cabinet. Cut the horizontal rails to fit between the stiles and fasten them as well. Now you are ready for drawers and doors (see pages 112–119).

Building a wall cabinet

Because it has no kick plate or drawers, a wall cabinet is easier to build than a base cabinet. It is essentially a rectangular box with shelves and a face frame. Build a standard wall cabinet 12 inches deep, including the stiles and rails but not including the doors.

Base cabinets usually have one fixed shelf, but wall cabinets work well with two or three adjustable shelves. Make scaled drawings, a cut list, and a cutting diagram (see page 46).

You'll Need

TIME: Several hours per cabinet.
SKILLS: Accurate planning, measuring, cutting, fastening.
TOOLS: Circular saw, drill, framing square, hammer.

Making the cabinet

Cut the sides to the total height of the cabinet. Install adjustable standards, or drill holes for shelf pins (see pages 20–21). For each sidepiece, cut a ¾×⅜-inch rabbet at the top, a ¾×⅜-inch dado for the bottom shelf, and a ¼×⅜-inch rabbet for the back panel (see pages 108–111).

Cut the bottom shelf and the top ¾ inch shorter than the width of the cabinet, and cut a ¼×⅜-inch rabbet in the rear of the top piece. Join the sides, the top piece, and the bottom shelf using 8d finishing nails and wood glue. Check for square as you assemble the parts.

Cut the back from ¼-inch plywood, ¾ inch narrower than the width of the cabinet and ⅜ inch shorter than the cabinet's height. Cut carefully so that all corners are square. Cut and fasten the top and bottom cleats. Squeeze wood glue onto the back rabbet and attach the back by driving 3d finishing nails every few inches.

Cut the stiles (the vertical pieces of the face frame) to the height of the cabinet and cut the rails (horizontal pieces) to fit between. Hold in place on the cabinet front to check the

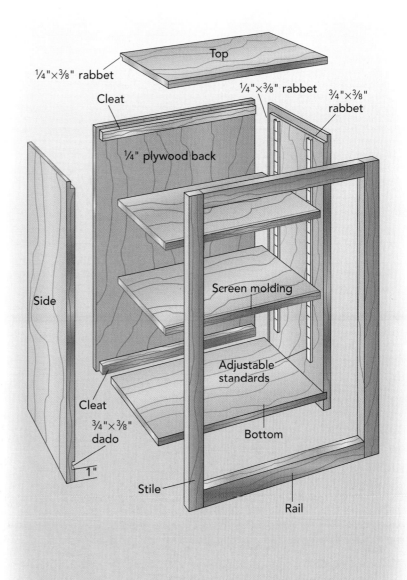

cuts; the stiles should extend ⅛ inch on each side. For the tightest joints, square up and glue the stiles and rails together before fastening them to the cabinet. Attach the completed face frame using wood glue and 8d finishing nails.

Cut shelves to fit inside the cabinet. Make them ⅛ inch shorter

than the width between the shelf supports so you can remove and reposition them easily. Cover the front edges of the shelves with screen molding (see page 120).

To build and install a cabinet door, see pages 112–117.

Building special base cabinets

Base cabinets hold a great deal because they are deep, but cookware and small appliances can get lost in the back corners. Plan for easy access. A narrow base cabinet works well for cookie sheets and baking pans, for instance. A simpler corner base that uses the walls for a back is shown on page 55. This version includes a finished back to cover imperfections in the wall.

You'll Need

TIME: A few hours.
SKILLS: Measuring, marking and cutting, fastening with screws.
TOOLS: Level, circular saw, framing square, drill.

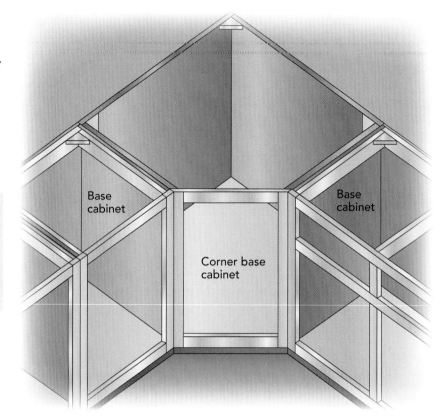

Base cabinet

Base cabinet

Corner base cabinet

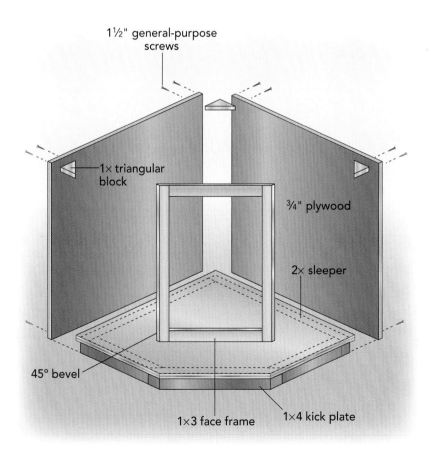

1½" general-purpose screws

1× triangular block

¾" plywood

2× sleeper

45° bevel

1×3 face frame

1×4 kick plate

Build a corner base cabinet

Set base cabinets in place on each side of the corner; level them and make sure they are level with each other, but do not attach them.

Cut ¾-inch plywood for the back and attach triangular blocks to the outside edge of each, near the top. Attach the backpieces to the wall. Cut a piece of plywood for the bottom. Cut 2× sleepers to the width needed to raise the bottom of the base to the same height as the adjoining cabinets. Screw the two rear sleepers to the backpieces and set the other two in place. Fasten the bottom to the sleepers with screws.

Cut a 1×4 to fit between the toe-kicks of the adjoining cabinets; make 45-degree bevel cuts at both ends. Attach it with screws. Position the adjoining cabinets against the corner base so the opening between them is square. Construct a face frame of 1×3s to fit tightly in the opening; bevel the outside edges 45 degrees. Attach the face by drilling pilot holes and driving screws.

Build a drawer base

A drawer base is similar to a standard base cabinet but with extra drawers and no doors. Most people prefer to have a larger drawer at the bottom. This version includes a pullout cutting board. You can build a large cabinet like the one shown on pages 46–48 and make one side a drawer base.

Make drawings and cut lists and construct the basic frame for the cabinet (see Steps 1–5 on pages 47–48). Install three front crosspieces; the two lower ones should be evenly spaced below the top one, while leaving a larger opening for the bottom drawer. Install nailers and drawer glides for all three drawers.

You don't want the cutting board to slide too smoothly, so provide two cleats on each side for the board to slide between. Make four cleats by rip-cutting pieces of 1× lumber to ¾ inch, so each is square in profile. Attach the cleats as shown, spacing them 1 inch apart.

Make the cutting board out of a hardwood, like maple. It should be ¼ inch narrower than the opening. Join two or three pieces side-by-side with blind dowels or biscuits (see pages 106–107). Then cut a front piece out of 1×2 and join it the same way. Attach a small wooden knob to the front of the cutting board using a double-threaded screw.

Cut stiles, square up, glue and clamp them together, and attach them with 8d finishing nails and wood glue. Position the stiles so they overlap the cabinet ⅛ inch on each side. Cut four rails to fit, and install them the same way. To build and install the drawers, see the instructions on pages 118–119.

Cutting board

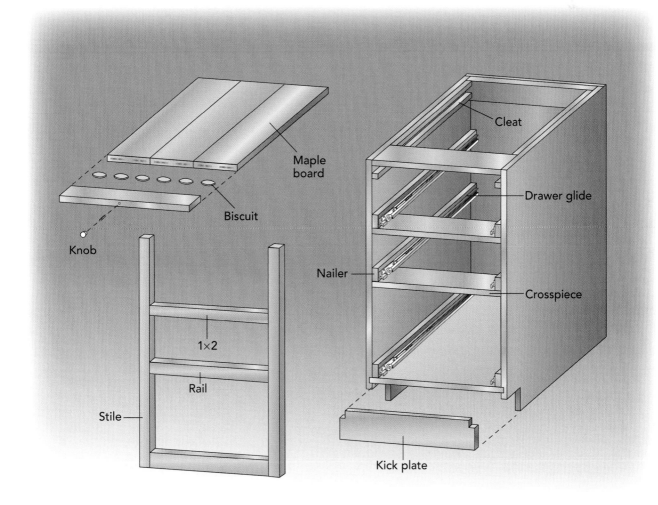

Maple board

Biscuit

Knob

1×2

Rail

Stile

Cleat

Drawer glide

Nailer

Crosspiece

Kick plate

Building a pantry cabinet

To maximize storage space in an area where you do not need a countertop, build a tall unit that mimics an old-fashioned pantry. This pantry cabinet has a tall space below that you can use as a broom closet; or install adjustable shelves. It is 24 inches deep, but a 12-inch unit will provide plenty of storage where space is at a premium. To store seldom-needed objects, build a pantry cabinet that extends all the way to the ceiling.

If the unit will stand next to standard base and wall cabinets with a countertop, plan so that the top doors match the wall cabinet doors. An 84-inch-tall pantry cabinet will be the same height as 30-inch-tall wall cabinets that are installed 18 inches above the countertop (see page 42).

This unit is made with many of the same techniques shown for a base cabinet (see pages 46–48).

Buy warp-free plywood for the doors and store the pieces flat before cutting. Edge the doors with veneer tape (see page 120) and surface mount trim with glue and brads. Use two catches for the lower doors, one near the bottom and one near the top, to help prevent them from warping over the years.

You'll Need

TIME: Most of a day.
SKILLS: Measuring and cutting, cutting dadoes, fastening with screws and nails.
TOOLS: Circular saw, drill, framing square, hammer.

Building a pantry unit

Cut the sides and make ³⁄₄×³⁄₈-inch dado cuts to receive three fixed shelves (see pages 108–111). Cut a ³⁄₈×³⁄₈-inch rabbet at the inside rear edge of each sidepiece. Install metal standards or drill holes for adjustable pins (see pages 20–21).

Cut the three shelves 1 inch shorter than the cabinet width. Working on a flat surface and checking for square, attach the shelves to the sidepieces with wood glue and 8d finishing nails. Cut a kick plate and attach it with glue and finishing nails. Cut 1×4 nailing cleats to fit between the sidepieces at the top and bottom and attach them to the sides.

Cut the back panel out of ¼-inch plywood, making sure each corner is square. Place it inside the rabbets and attach it with wood glue and 3d finishing nails every few inches. Attach the stiles with glue and 8d finishing nails so that they extend past the sidepieces ⅛ inch on each side. Cut and attach rails to fit between them.

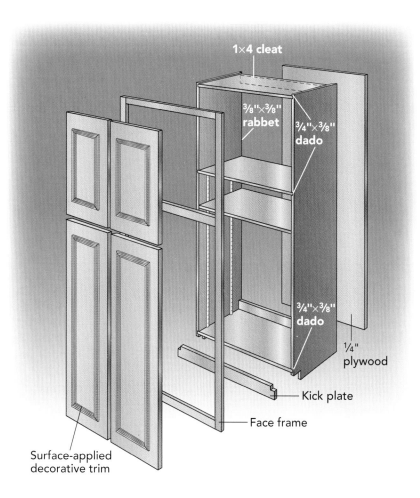

1×4 cleat

³⁄₈"×³⁄₈" rabbet

³⁄₄"×³⁄₈" dado

³⁄₄"×³⁄₈" dado

¼" plywood

Kick plate

Face frame

Surface-applied decorative trim

Making an adjustable spice rack

Adjustable shelves make this more versatile than the usual spice rack. An open rack located near the stove will be convenient while cooking. Many spice containers, bottles of oil, and condiment jars are attractive enough to display.

Choose a hardwood lumber and plywood, and stain it to match your kitchen cabinets; or use softwood, and paint it with several coats of gloss or semigloss enamel.

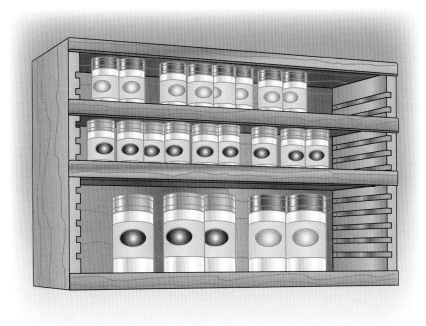

You'll Need

TIME: Half a day.
SKILLS: Measuring and cutting, cutting dadoes, fastening with screws and nails.
TOOLS: Circular saw, clamp, drill, framing square, hammer.

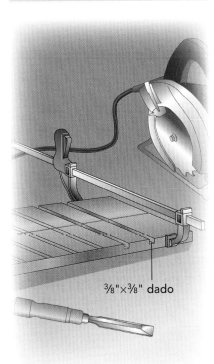

⅜"×⅜" dado

¾"×⅜" rabbet

¼" plywood back

⅜" plywood

¾" lattice

1. Cut and dado the sides.

Cut two pieces of 1×4 to the height of the unit, minus ¾ inch. Clamp them together and cut ⅜×⅜-inch dadoes every 2 inches. At the top and bottom, leave 2 inches clear. Cut pieces of 1×4 for the top and bottom and cut ¾×⅜-inch rabbets at both ends of each.

2. Assemble the parts.

Apply wood glue and clamp the top and bottom pieces to the sidepieces, checking for square. When the glue is dry, cut a piece of ¼-inch plywood, ¼ inch shorter and narrower than the unit. Attach it to the back with wood glue and 3d finishing nails.

3. Make the shelves.

Cut strips of ⅜-inch plywood, 3½ inches wide, to fit. Measure from dado to dado for the correct length. Glue pieces of ¾-inch lattice molding (which is ¼ inch thick) to the front edge of the shelves, overhanging the shelf edge by about ⅛ inch on each side.

Installing kitchen cabinets

Install cabinets after you complete the rough plumbing and electrical wiring and install the flooring. Patch and prime the walls and put on the first coat of wall paint before installing cabinets.

If you purchased your cabinets ready-made, inspect them carefully before installing. It is not unusual to find imperfections. Before installing base cabinets, use a level to find the highest point of the floor and begin the layout from there. When installing wall cabinets, work with a helper and a stable ladder so one person can hold a cabinet in perfect alignment while the other drives screws. Attach cabinets with screws driven at least 2 inches into studs.

You'll Need

TIME: A full day to install about a dozen cabinets.
SKILLS: Leveling, measuring, attaching with screws.
TOOLS: Level, drill, hammer, clamps, chisel.

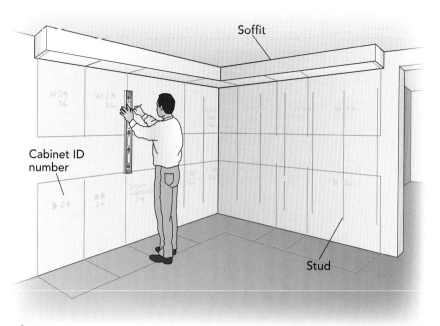

Soffit
Cabinet ID number
Stud

1. Lay out the cabinets.

Installation will go smoothly and you'll have fewer mishaps if you mark the wall to show where each cabinet will go. Also, draw lines to show the stud locations. (Draw lightly wherever your marks will not be covered by a cabinet.) Remove any moldings or other obstructions that would keep cabinets from fitting tightly against the wall.

Soffit
Shim
Temporary brace

2. Install wall cabinets.

Begin in a corner. Make sure that the first wall cabinet is plumb in all directions; use shims if necessary. Drive screws into studs to attach. Secure other cabinets to the wall and to each other (see Step 5).

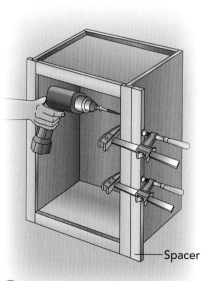

Spacer

3. Use a spacer at the end.

At the end of a wall, you may have to rip-cut a spacer at an angle to make it fit snugly. Test-fit the final cabinet and spacer. Clamp the spacer while you drill pilot holes and drive screws.

Experts' Insight
Plumb and level

If the walls or floors are not level or plumb, you may be tempted to install cabinets out of level. This is a bad idea: If you start out wrong, the misalignments will be compounded and impossible to correct later. If the floor is wavy or out of level, install vinyl cove base to cover up the gap at the bottom of base cabinets. Or you can remove the kick plates and reinstall them tight to the floor after the cabinets are installed.

Shim

Middle stile

Shim

4. Level and attach base cabinets.

Starting in a corner, set the first base cabinet in place and use shims at the floor or wall (or both) to make it level and plumb in all directions. The cabinet should be resting firmly, with no wobbles, before you attach it. Drive screws through the rear ledger and into studs. Recheck for level and plumb; driving the screws can move the cabinet a bit.

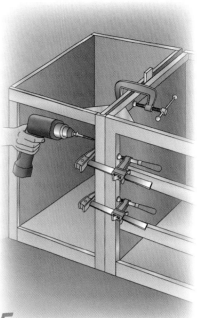

5. Join cabinets together.

Clamp cabinets together so the stiles are flush and join them by drilling pilot holes and driving screws. Use a chisel to nip off shims that stick out.

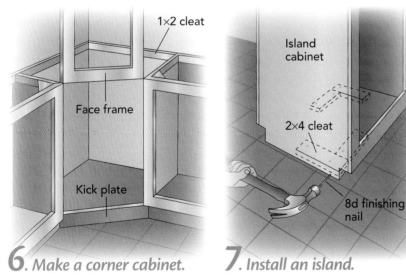

1×2 cleat

Face frame

Kick plate

Island cabinet

2×4 cleat

8d finishing nail

6. Make a corner cabinet.

If the walls are in good condition, buy a knock-down corner unit like this, or make your own (see page 50 for a unit with backing). Install the base first, aligning the kick plate with those adjoining. Join the face frame to the adjoining cabinets and install 1×2 cleats on the walls.

7. Install an island.

If a cabinet does not attach to a wall, provide framing on the floor. Measure the inside of the cabinet bottom, and attach 2×4 cleats to the floor so the cabinet can slip over them and fit snugly. Drill pilot holes and drive finishing nails or attach with screws and cover the heads with molding.

Improving kitchen cabinets

Adequate storage capacity is often undone by awkward access; canned goods get buried, pots and pans get jumbled together. By adding a pullout drawer, a door-mounted shelf, or small open shelves, you will greatly improve your cabinet's efficiency. Home centers and kitchen supply sources carry many coated-wire racks and shelves, as well as slide-out drawers, that can easily be attached to cabinet doors and floors. Here are three solutions that you can add to new or existing cabinets.

You'll Need

Time: About half a day for each project.
Skills: Measuring, squaring, cutting dadoes, attaching with screws and nails.
Tools: Circular saw, jigsaw, drill, hammer, square, chisel.

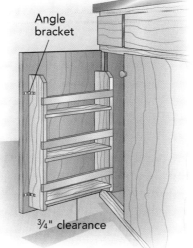

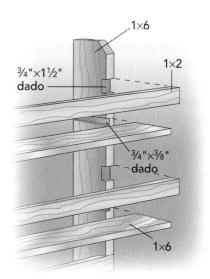

Door-mounted shelves

To store small items within easy reach, build shelves for the door. Allow at least ¾ inch clearance all around the door so the shelves will not bump into the cabinet frame.

Cut the sidepieces and make dadoes for the shelves and the fronts. Join the pieces by drilling pilot holes, applying glue, and driving in 4d finishing nails. Anchor the unit with screws and angle brackets.

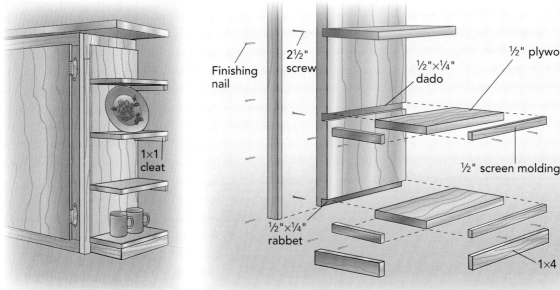

Side-of-cabinet open shelves

This simple design uses 1×1 cleats against the wall for extra support. Use plywood and cover the edges with molding or veneer tape, or purchase ½-inch-thick lumber for the shelves.

To build the shelves, cut ½×¼-inch dadoes in the upright support (see pages 108–111). Cut the shelves and attach them in the dadoes with glue and 2½-inch screws driven through the back of the support into the shelves. Drill pilot holes; drive the screws carefully. Cover the shelf edges with ½-inch screen molding and the support edge with ¾-inch screen molding. Mount the unit by driving screws from inside the cabinet.

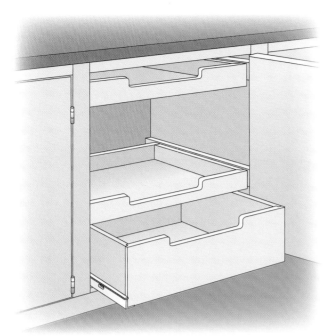

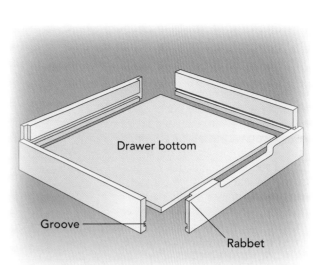

Drawer bottom

Groove

Rabbet

Roll-out drawers

Drawers like these greatly increase base cabinet efficiency, allowing you to reach pots and pans, lids, and small appliances at the back of the cabinet without getting down on your knees. Begin by measuring the width of the opening and subtracting the thickness of the drawer glides you'll use. Ready-to-install drawers are available at home centers, or you can build your own.

1. Cut the pieces.

Cut 1×4 sides 22 inches long and cut ½×⅜-inch grooves, with the bottom of the grooves ¾ inch up from the bottom edge (see pages 108–111). Cut a front and back piece, each to the width of the drawer. Cut grooves in these pieces to match the grooves in the sidepieces. Also cut ⅜×¾-inch rabbets on the inside ends of the front and back. Use a jigsaw to cut a decorative scallop in the front piece. Cut a piece of ½-inch plywood to fit inside the grooves of the side, back, and front pieces. Install any nailer needed for the glide.

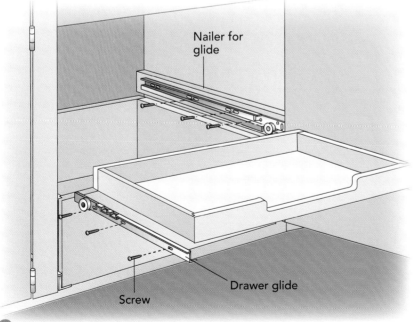

Nailer for glide

Drawer glide

Screw

Experts' Insight

Getting the right drawer sizes

Before you start building a slide-out drawer for a base cabinet, make sure that it will slide out without bumping into the doors. Some doors provide an opening just as big as the cabinet frame when they open; others provide less space.

If you need to narrow the drawer so that it can slide past the door, you may need to increase the thickness of the glide nailer inside the cabinet. Add a strip of ½-inch plywood behind the nailer.

2. Assemble and install.

Dry-fit all the pieces to make sure that all the joints will be snug. Apply glue to the rabbets (but not to the grooves), drill pilot holes, and attach all the joints with 4d finishing nails. Attach nailers to the insides of the cabinets, and install glides on both the nailers and the drawer (see page 119).

Lighting for cabinets

Undercabinet lighting will brighten any gloomy kitchen. This added illumination can make food preparation more enjoyable and make a small room seem larger. Place undercabinet and cove lights so they will be out of sight; they should illuminate, not glare. Low-voltage halogen lights are the easiest to install if cabinets are already in place. If adding new cabinets, consider running cables and installing fluorescent lights.

You'll Need

TIME: A couple of hours for a set of halogens; running cable for fluorescent lights takes longer.
SKILLS: Basic wiring.
TOOLS: Drill, lineman's pliers, keyhole or reciprocating saw, screwdriver.

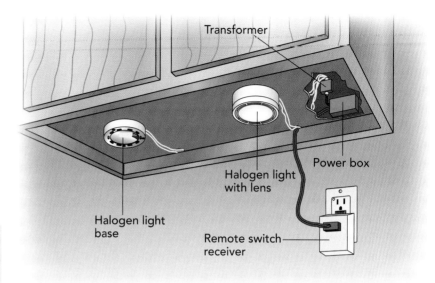

Transformer

Power box

Halogen light with lens

Halogen light base

Remote switch receiver

1. Plan for a halogen system.

Map out the job and purchase a set of halogen undercabinet lights with all the lights and wire you need. These lights get very hot, so place them away from combustible materials and out of the reach of children. Drill inconspicuous holes and run the thin wire into the cabinet. Install the power box and transformer out of sight. Run the power cord from a receptacle to the transformer. Coil any excess wire and tuck it out of the way.

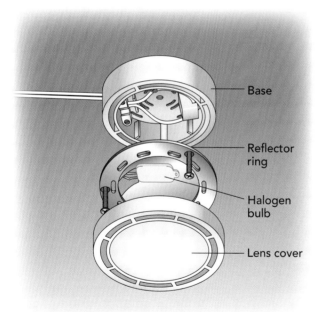

Base

Reflector ring

Halogen bulb

Lens cover

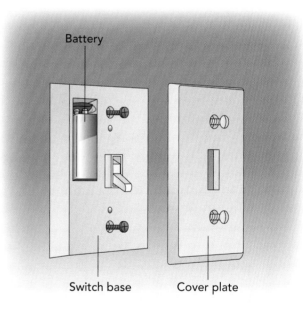

Battery

Switch base

Cover plate

2. Install the lights.

Disassemble a light and attach the fixture base to the underside of the cabinet with short screws; make sure they do not poke through the wood into the cabinet interior. Connect the wires in the light and staple down running wire. Install the reflector ring and plug in the bulb. Install the lens cover.

3. Connect the switch.

The switch operates by battery and is mounted flush to the wall, so you can easily place it anywhere on a wall or cabinet. Screw the housing to the wall by driving screws into a stud. Or drill holes in the wall surface, tap in plastic anchors, and drive screws into the anchors. Attach the cover plate to the housing.

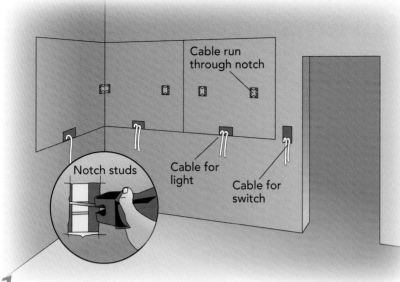

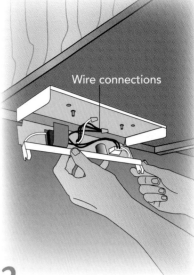

1. Run cable for fluorescent lights.

Hire an electrician if you do not know how to run power from a box. With the cabinets removed, mark the walls carefully to show where the cables will emerge from the wall. (Disassemble the lights to find out exactly where the cable will enter them.) Plan to pull the cables through the lower rear lip of the cabinet if it has one, or right below the bottom of the cabinet.

Run power to the switch, then to the first light; run a cable out of the first light to the second and so on until you come to the last light. To run the cable past studs, cut holes in the wallboard or plaster and make notches with a reciprocating saw. These holes will be covered by the cabinets.

If the cabinets have lower lips, drill holes or cut notches for the cable. Install the cabinets.

2. Connect the lights.

For each light, punch out the knockout and install a cable clamp. Run the cable into the fixture and screw the fixture to the cabinet. Strip and connect wires. Attach the cover plate and install a fluorescent bulb. Turn on the power and test. If the light is glaring at eye level, install a strip of wood in front to deflect the glare downward.

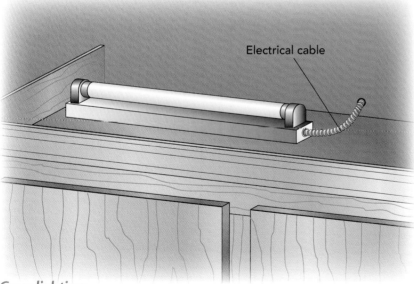

Cove lighting

Subtle light from the top of a cabinet gently illuminates the room. Set fluorescent fixtures on top of your cabinets and make sure they are not visible to people standing in the room. (Because the wires and fixtures are hidden from view, you are not as restricted with the installation.) You may want to add cove molding on top of the cabinets to help hide the lights.

Run electrical cable from a switch to the area above the cabinets. Hook up the lights. Usually you can let them sit on top of the cabinet.

Experts' Insight
Lighting a kitchen

Most well-lighted kitchens have these types of lights:
- Overhead or cove lighting that provides general illumination for the whole room. A kitchen should have at least 300 watts of incandescent lighting.
- Undercabinet lights. These are essential because you stand between overhead lights and a countertop. Plan for one 20-watt fluorescent light or one 12-watt halogen light for every 3 feet of countertop length.
- Accent lights for special areas. Direct some track lights toward the sink, for instance, or hang a light above a dining area.

Chapter Three

Projects

This chapter includes nine storage and shelving projects you can build, ranging from entertainment centers to a wine rack. They are all designed to be easy to build and adaptable to many different situations.

In addition to the projects in this chapter, instructions for basic storage and shelving construction are shown on pages 12–33. And you'll find kitchen cabinets and other kitchen projects on pages 42–59.

For custom storage solutions, you can alter the projects in this book to fit specific needs or use them as the basis for your own designs. Combining elements from several designs will often result in an ideal solution to storage needs.

BUILDING A PROJECT

Before you start a project, take a moment to go over the instructions. Determine the dimensions for the project where needed, and make a list of the tools and materials you will need.

If the project calls for techniques you aren't familiar with, check pages 96–121 to see what's involved. Where a project calls for a tool you don't have, you can usually rent it. (Many do-it-yourselfers, however, see such a situation as a perfect excuse to buy the tool. After all, if you need it now, you will probably need it again.)

Refer to the chapters on tools and materials and basic skills when you are unsure how to use a tool or perform a task.

Building adjustable entertainment shelves

These shelves have an informal look, but if you finish them with a glossy coat of enamel paint or build them with hardwood plywood and stain them, they will be classy enough for most living rooms.

The shelves are made of plywood, cut at a gentle curve and edged with veneer tape. The standards are made of 2-inch galvanized conduit, the kind used for heavy-duty outdoor electrical installations. Conduit couplings slip over the conduit to support the shelves.

You'll Need

TIME: Several hours, plus time for painting or finishing.
SKILLS: Measuring and cutting curves, cutting metal conduit.
TOOLS: Jigsaw, drill, hammer, framing square, hacksaw.

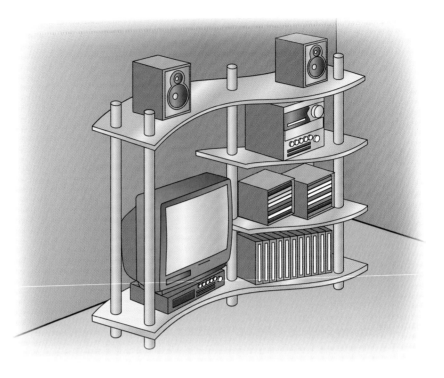

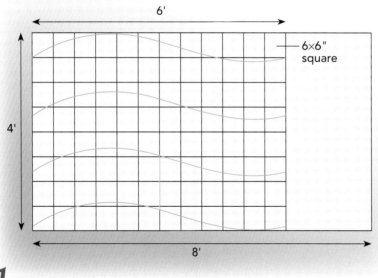

1. Cut the shelves.

On a sheet of plywood, draw lines for a 6-foot-long, 14-inch-wide curved shelf. Use a framing square and pencil to divide part of the plywood sheet into a grid of 6-inch squares. Then draw the top curve, using the illustration above as a guide. Experiment until it looks smooth and even. Draw the second line parallel with the first line and mark for a square cutoff.

Cut the first shelf with a jigsaw and sand the edges smooth. Use the first shelf as a template and draw the next two shelves. Use the framing square to draw a line dividing one of the shelves in half, then cut the shelves.

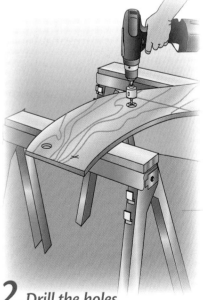

2. Drill the holes.

On one of the shelves, mark for centers of holes 3 inches in from each corner. Mark for another hole in the center of the shelf's width and 33 inches from one end. Drill with a 2-inch hole saw, then use the shelf as a template to mark for holes in the other shelves.

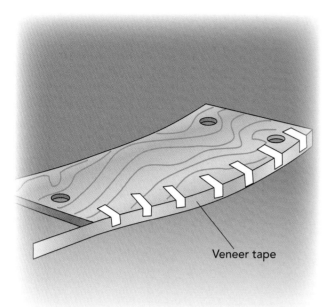

Veneer tape

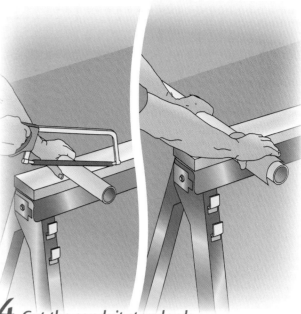

3. Apply edging.

Cover the plywood edges with veneer tape. Attach it by applying glue to the plywood edge and holding the veneer tape in place with masking tape (see page 120).

4. Cut the conduit standards.

Cut five pieces of 2-inch conduit (the nonthreaded kind) to 54 inches or so, depending on how tall you want the unit to be. Use a hacksaw or a tubing cutter. To prepare the pipe for painting, first sand the conduit with a loose sheet of medium-grit sandpaper.

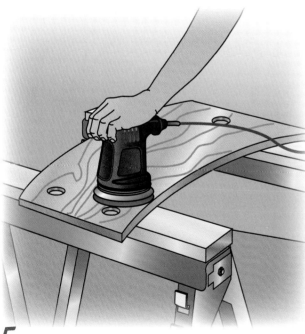

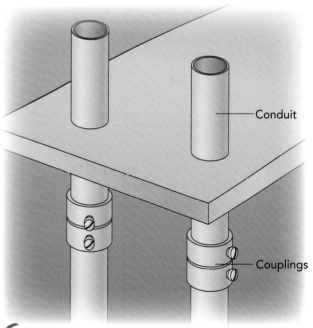

Conduit

Couplings

5. Sand and paint standards and shelves.

Sand the shelves smooth. Apply a coat of primer and two coats of enamel paint to conduit, couplings, and shelves. If you like the silvery look of galvanized conduit and couplings, just leave them alone; the finish will last.

6. Slip on shelves, attach couplings.

At the bottom of each standard, slip on a coupling and tighten the setscrews. Slip the bottom shelf onto all five standards and slide it down. Slip on couplings for the next shelf and measure to see that they are all at the same height. Slip on the shelf. Repeat for all the shelves. If the standards fit tightly into the holes, the unit will be stable. If it wobbles, anchor it to a wall with angle brackets and screws.

Building an entertainment center

This handsome unit hides a TV and a stereo behind cabinet doors and includes shelves for media storage or display.

The central cabinet has adjustable shelves 2 feet wide—large enough for standard stereo components and a medium-sized TV. Shallow shelves in the middle unit leave space at the rear for wires and ventilation. The doors shown are slabs trimmed with half-round molding, but you could make panel doors instead (see pages 112–113).

You'll Need

TIME: Two days.
SKILLS: Making doors, measuring and cutting, cutting dadoes.
TOOLS: Circular saw, drill, hammer, framing square.

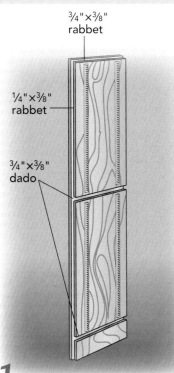

¾"×⅜" rabbet

¼"×⅜" rabbet

¾"×⅜" dado

1. Make the side panels.

Cut two pieces of ¾-inch plywood to 22×80 inches. Cut a ¾×⅜-inch rabbet at the top and a ¼×⅜-inch rabbet at one edge of each (make the panels mirror images of each other). Cut two ¾×⅜-inch dadoes (see pages 108–111). Attach metal shelving standards (see page 20).

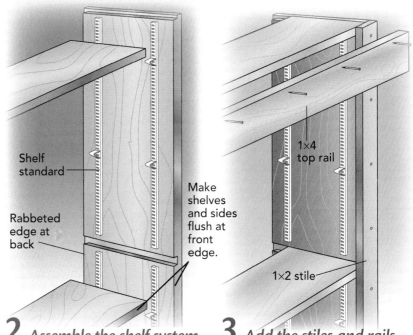

Shelf standard

Rabbeted edge at back

Make shelves and sides flush at front edge.

1×4 top rail

1×2 stile

2. Assemble the shelf system.

Cut three ¾-inch plywood shelves 18×24 inches and apply screen molding to the front edges (see page 120). Attach the shelves into the top rabbet and the dadoes with glue and 6d finishing nails. Cut ¼-inch plywood for the back; attach it in the back rabbet with 3d finishing nails.

3. Add the stiles and rails.

Cut two 1×2 stiles and attach them with glue and 6d finishing nails, allowing the outside edges to overhang the plywood by ⅛ inch. Cut rails—1×6 for the bottom, 1×2 for the middle, and 1×4 for the top—to fit between the stiles and attach them the same way.

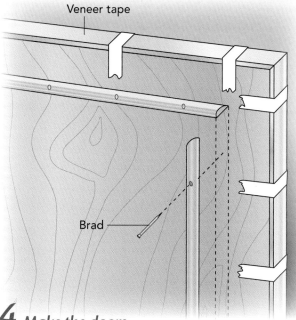

4. Make the doors.

To make trimmed slab doors, start with warp-free plywood. Select a door and hinge style (see pages 114–116) and cut the doors to size. Take into account the molding you will use for the bottom and top. Apply veneer tape to the edges (see page 120). Trim the door by attaching miter-cut pieces of molding with glue and small brads.

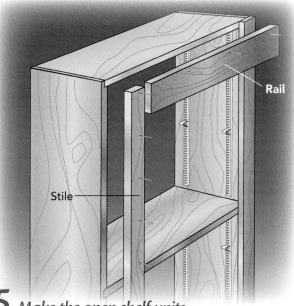

5. Make the open shelf units.

Cut four plywood sidepieces to the same height as the side panels (Step 1) but only 12 inches deep. Cut rabbets and dadoes and install the metal shelf standards as shown in Step 1. Cut three shelves and assemble the units as in Step 2. Add stiles and rails as in Step 3, except install them flush against the edges that will adjoin the middle unit.

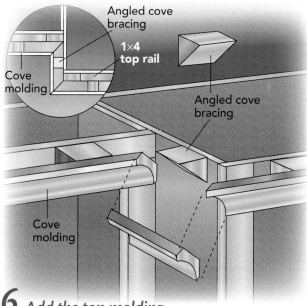

6. Add the top molding.

Attach the open shelf units to the middle unit with 1¼-inch screws, and attach the entire unit to the wall by driving screws through the back panel and into studs. Trim the top with cove molding. Rip angled bracing from a 2×2 to back the molding. Make miter cuts for the outside corners (see inset) and coped joints for the inside corners (see page 100).

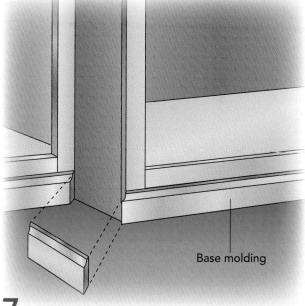

7. Install the base molding and finish.

To make the unit appear built-in, purchase molding that matches the base molding in the room. Install it the way you did the top molding (Step 6). Cut the adjustable shelves to size. Apply a coat of primer and two coats of enamel paint to all parts or apply stain followed by polyurethane finish if you used hardwood plywood. Then install the doors (see pages 114–117).

Adding a radiator cover

A steam or hot-water radiator can be an eyesore. This cover hides a radiator under an attractive shelf and makes it more efficient because of the heat-reflecting metal surfaces above and behind the radiator. The spaces above and below the front panel cause warm air to move away from the radiator via convection: Cold air enters from below, and warm air rises out the top. To match the style of your room, you could make the front and sides with louvers or slats instead of perforated metal.

You'll Need

TIME: Most of a day.
SKILLS: Measuring and cutting, connecting with screws.
TOOLS: Circular saw, drill, hammer, utility knife, square, level, staple gun, tin snips.

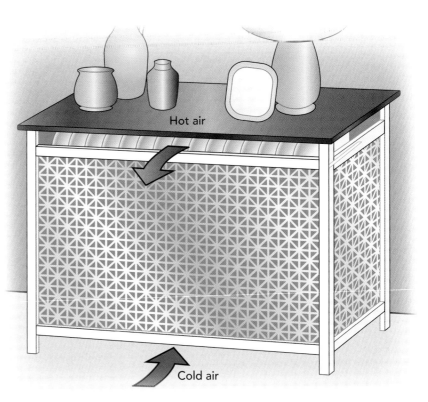

Hot air

Cold air

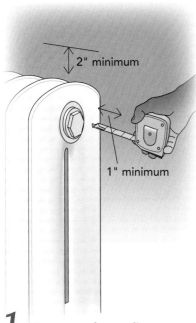

2" minimum

1" minimum

1. Measure the radiator.

The radiator cover should be at least 2 inches above the top of the radiator and at least 1 inch from the sides and front. If you turn the radiator handle often, leave an access space so you won't have to remove the whole cover to reach the handle.

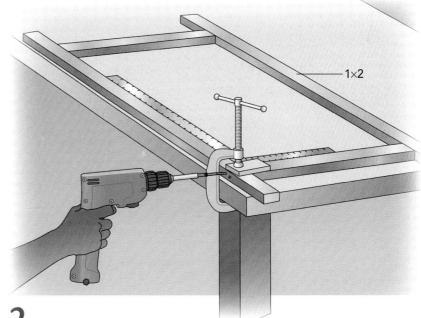

1×2

2. Assemble the frame.

For each side, cut two upright 1×2s. Cut two horizontal 1×2 rails 3 inches shorter than the frame will be. For each end (you may need only one end if the radiator side is against a wall) cut two horizontals 3¾ inches shorter than the frame width.

Assemble the frames, providing a 3-inch space at the floor and a 2-inch space at the top. Drill pilot holes and drive 3-inch trim head screws, or fasten with dowels (see pages 106–107). If the cover is longer than 3 feet, install an intermediate upright so the metal grid doesn't sag. Paint the frames.

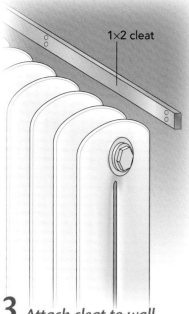

1×2 cleat

3. Attach cleat to wall.

To add strength to the top, install a cleat on the wall for the top to rest on. Position the frames where they will go and use a level to mark lines between them. Attach a 1×2 cleat by drilling pilot holes and driving 2-inch screws into the studs.

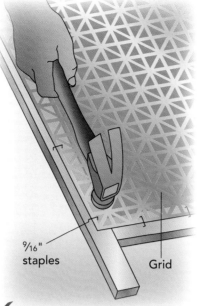

$^{9}/_{16}$" staples

Grid

4. Attach metal grid.

Purchase sheets of perforated sheet metal; "union jack" is a popular pattern. Cut the sheets 1½ inches longer than the openings. Center them on the back of the frames and attach with $^{9}/_{16}$-inch staples every inch or so. You may have to finish driving the staples with a hammer.

Foil backing

5. Install insulating backing.

Purchase insulating foil, which comes in rolls. Cut it with a utility knife and staple it to the wall(s) behind the radiator with a staple gun. If you have plaster walls, you may need to fasten the foil to 1×2 cleats screwed into wall studs.

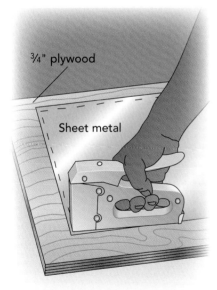

¾" plywood

Sheet metal

6. Attach undershelf metal.

Cut the top out of ¾-inch plywood; it should overhang the frame an inch or so. Cut a piece of sheet metal that will fit inside the frame top opening and attach it to the underside of the top with staples.

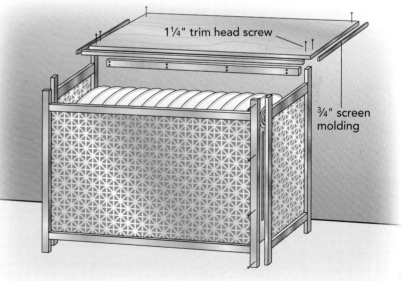

1¼" trim head screw

¾" screen molding

7. Assemble the parts.

Join the front frame piece to the endpiece(s) by drilling pilot holes and driving 1¼-inch trim head screws. Place the frame pieces next to the radiator. Attach the top to the frame with 1¼-inch trim head screws, then attach it to the wall cleat in the same way. Cover the plywood edges of the top with ¾-inch screen molding (see page 120). Apply a final coat of paint, being careful not to paint the reflective metal.

Installing closet organizers

A standard closet, with a single rod and shelf, wastes valuable space. Improve your usable storage by dividing a closet into sections tailored to suit your needs.

Divide hanging clothes into two or three groups according to height. Determine how much width each group requires; make sure the clothes will not be crammed together. Figure how much shelf space you need for sweaters, as well as rack space for shoes. You may want to purchase plastic storage boxes that fit on the shelves. Allow extra room for future purchases.

Diagram of your shelf system on graph paper, and make a materials list. Use ¾-inch plywood and edging for the shelves and upright supports (see the box on page 69 for typical shelf measurements). Use 1×2 for cleats and heel stops, 1¼-inch dowels for hanging rods, metal standards and clips for the shelves, and hardware to hold rods.

Cut the uprights for the tower of shelves and install metal standards for adjustable shelves (see page 20). Fasten the fixed shelves with glue and 8d finishing nails. Position the shelf unit, check it for square, and attach it to the wall with angle brackets and screws.

Cut the top shelf to fit between the sidewalls and the middle shelf to fit to the shelf tower. Attach 1×2 cleats to the wall and attach the shelves to the cleats. Cut and install closet rods using special closet-rod hardware. Cut and attach shoe shelves at about a 30-degree angle and nail 1×2s for heel stops.

You'll Need

Time: A full day.
Skills: Measuring and cutting, leveling, attaching with nails.
Tools: Circular saw, level, drill, hacksaw, hammer, square.

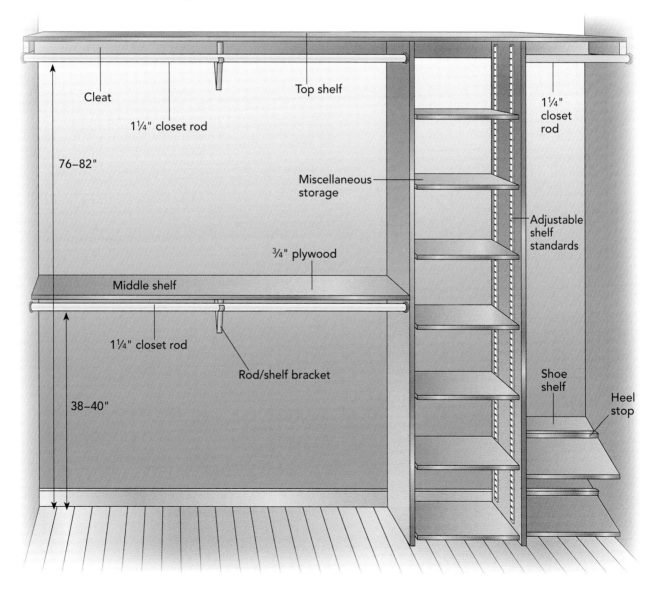

- Cleat
- 1¼" closet rod
- 76–82"
- Top shelf
- 1¼" closet rod
- Miscellaneous storage
- Adjustable shelf standards
- ¾" plywood
- Middle shelf
- 1¼" closet rod
- Rod/shelf bracket
- 38–40"
- Shoe shelf
- Heel stop

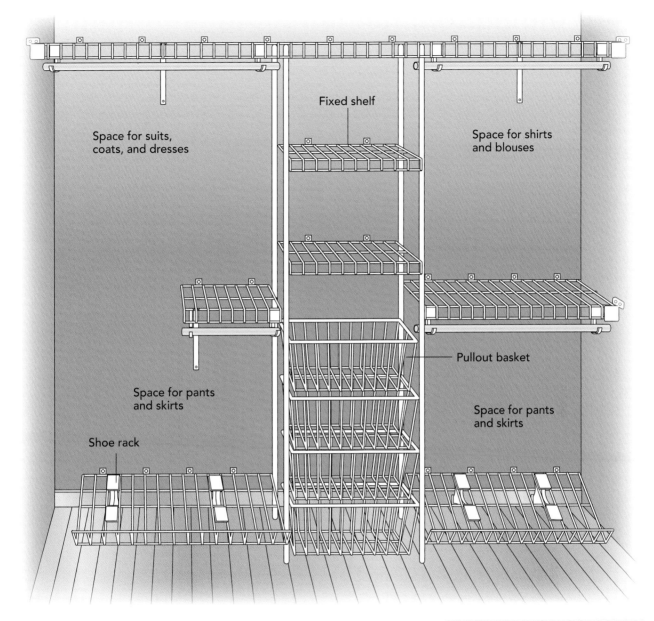

Space for suits, coats, and dresses

Fixed shelf

Space for shirts and blouses

Pullout basket

Space for pants and skirts

Space for pants and skirts

Shoe rack

Wire closet organizers are easy to install, need no painting, and often cost less than the materials to build wood shelves. You may be able to buy a kit that fits your closet with little cutting.

Make a drawing with exact dimensions and take it to a home center to buy the parts. You'll need shelves with hanger rods, wall-hanging clips, end clips, diagonal supports for shelves more than 2 feet long, and rubber caps to cover any exposed metal rod ends. You may also want a drawer unit.

Install the drawer tower first; then cut shelves to fit above and on both

sides of it. Draw level lines on the walls, install the clips so they are level, and then snap the shelves into the clips.

Install wall-hanging clips at the rear wall. Some types of anchors may not hold securely in drywall. Mount hardware to wall studs when possible, or use expanding anchors that grip the drywall. Install end wall clips at the sidewalls.

Cut the shelves to length with a hacksaw or bolt cutters. After snapping the shelves in place, install shelf supports.

MEASUREMENTS
Common closet sizes

A closet for hanging clothes is usually 24 inches deep. Make shelves 18 inches deep. Shirts, blouses, and skirts usually require 36 vertical inches. For men's and women's suits and slacks, allow 42 inches. Coats and dresses usually need 54 inches. Robes and long dresses may require up to 68 inches.

Making a desk and organizer

A flush door (one that is smooth, without any panels) makes a serviceable desk surface when placed on a pair of two-drawer filing cabinets. If it is made of oak or birch, you can stain it and apply a coat of polyurethane instead of applying laminate. The handy shelf system shown above the desk requires careful planning and plenty of dado cuts.

You'll Need

TIME: A day to make both pieces.
SKILLS: Measuring and cutting, cutting dadoes, gluing and trimming plastic laminate.
TOOLS: Circular saw, square, paintbrush, laminate roller, laminate trimmer or router, sanding block.

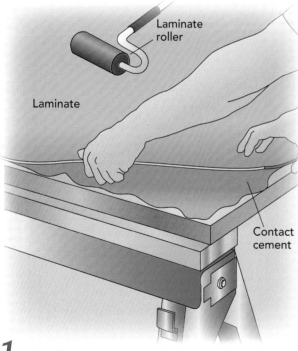

1. Glue laminate onto the door.

Cut a piece of plastic laminate about an inch wider and longer than the door. To prevent cracks, score the cutline with a knife before cutting. Use a paintbrush to spread an even coat of contact cement to the back of the laminate and the face of the door. Allow it to dry. With a helper carefully place the laminate on the door so that all of the door is covered; once placed, you cannot budge it. Use a laminate roller or rolling pin to ensure bonding.

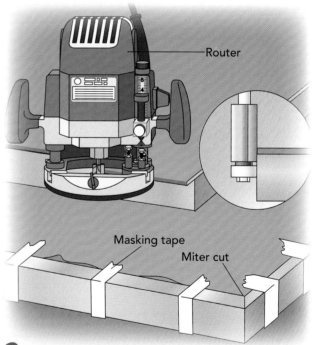

2. Trim and edge the door.

Trim overhanging laminate so its edge is flush with the door edge using a laminate trimmer or a router equipped with a laminate-trimming bit (see inset). Clean up rough edges with a sanding block.

Edge the door with 1×2 hardwood. Miter-cut the corners and attach the edging with wood glue. Tape the edging in place until the glue dries (see page 120).

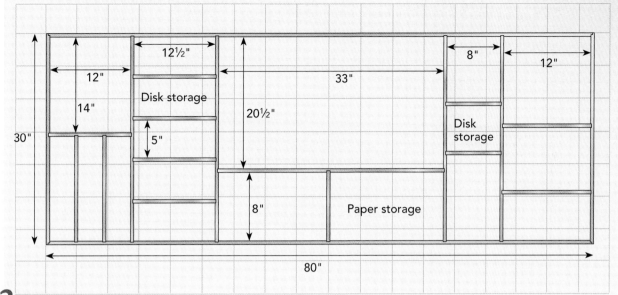

3. Plan the shelf system.

On a sheet of graph paper, draw a complete plan of the shelf system. The plan shown above has several compartments for full sheets of paper as well as compartments for CDs and computer disks. Make the spaces an inch or so wider than the items to be stored.

Make the shelf unit at least 11 inches deep to accommodate full sheets of paper. To figure the exact size of each piece, take into account the thickness of the plywood—½ inch—as well as the ¼-inch-deep dadoes. Double-check your figures; it's easy to make a mistake.

4. Cut and assemble the shelves.

Cut the top and bottom pieces and cut ½x¼-inch dadoes and rabbets to accept the uprights (see pages 108–111). Cut the vertical shelf supports to length and cut dadoes to receive the shelves. Saw the larger shelves, cutting dadoes where necessary.

Temporarily assemble the pieces by pushing them into place and double-check measurements for the smaller pieces. Assemble with wood glue and 3d finishing nails. Cut ¼-inch plywood for the back and attach it with glue and 3d finishing nails. Paint the interior to match the desktop laminate.

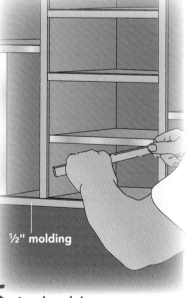

5. Apply edging.

Cut pieces of ½-inch molding to cover the plywood edges. Install the two long horizontal pieces first, then all the vertical pieces, then the remaining horizontals. Use wood glue to avoid nailing; hold the edging in position with strips of masking tape until the glue dries.

Adding a window seat

With open shelves on both sides, this seat makes a flat window feel like a bay window. A seat 20 inches deep affords ample room for lounging. Two large drawers underneath are handy for storing linens, and the shelves hold a small collection of books, making this a cozy reading nook.

Begin by removing base molding from the wall; cut and reinstall it on the uncovered wall sections after installing the unit. Mark studs so you can install brackets for holding the shelves and seat in place (see page 12).

You'll Need

TIME: A day to build and paint.
SKILLS: Cutting dadoes and rabbets, squaring, attaching with nails and screws.
TOOLS: Circular saw, jigsaw, drill, hammer, square, level.

1. Build the box and face frame.

From ¾-inch plywood, cut two sidepieces, a top piece, and a backpiece to the dimensions shown. Working on a flat surface, fasten the back to the sidepieces by driving 2-inch screws through the back and into the sides.

Cut 1×4 and 1×2 rails and stiles to the dimensions shown. Position the bottom rail so it runs past the box sides ¼ inch on each side and so the center piece is in its exact middle. Attach by drilling pilot holes, applying wood glue, and driving 6d finishing nails. Attach the stiles and the top rail in the same way; the top rail will be 1½ inches above the plywood pieces. Cut a top piece to fit and attach it with wood glue and 6d finishing nails. Cut four strips for the glide supports and attach them with 1¼-inch screws.

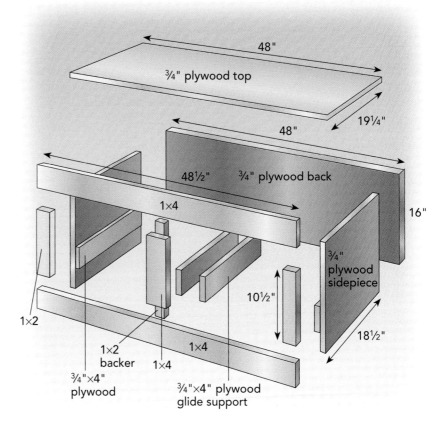

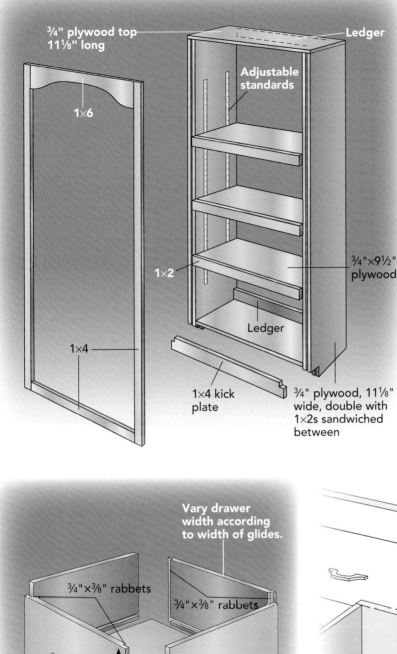

¾" plywood top
11⅛" long

Ledger

Adjustable standards

1×6

1×2

¾"×9½" plywood

Ledger

1×4

1×4 kick plate

¾" plywood, 11⅛" wide, double with 1×2s sandwiched between

2. Build the shelves.

Decide on the height and width of the shelf units; in a narrow room with a low ceiling, you can run them to the sidewalls and from floor to ceiling. Make each shelf standard of two pieces of ¾-inch plywood, 11⅛ inches wide, with two 1×2s sandwiched in between (see pages 24–25). If you choose to support the shelves with dowels or pins, bore holes now (see page 21). (Metal standards can be installed later.) Build each shelf unit by first attaching one standard to the window seat using 3½-inch screws. Plumb it and attach it to the rear wall using angle brackets, then install the second standard. Install the kick plate and bottom shelf. Prefab the face frame, joining the pieces with glue and dowels (see page 106). Install the face frame by drilling pilot holes and driving 1⅝-inch trim head screws every 6 inches. Build the shelves using ¾×9½-inch-wide plywood with 1×2 edging.

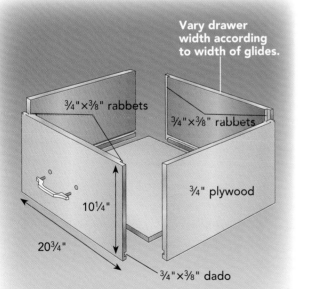

Vary drawer width according to width of glides.

¾"×⅜" rabbets

¾"×⅜" rabbets

¾" plywood

10¼"

20¾"

¾"×⅜" dado

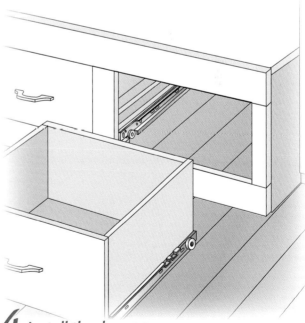

3. Build the drawers.

Measure the openings in the base unit and build drawers to fit (see pages 118–119). Use ¾-inch plywood for all the pieces. Check the drawer glides to see how much smaller than the opening the drawers should be. Install the drawer pull.

4. Install the drawers.

Attach drawer glides to the drawers and to the drawer unit (see page 119) and slide in the drawers.

Give the entire unit two coats of enamel paint, or stain it and apply a polyurethane finish. Have a cushion (or cushions) made by an upholsterer.

Adding wraparound shelves

In rooms where every square inch counts, shelves set well above the floor make sense. Combine them with overhead shelves set around the perimeter of the room, and you can equip a small space with a surprising amount of shelf area. You don't even need generous ceiling height: The most compact ranch home has enough room for one shelf set above the door and window casing.

You'll Need

Time: A day to install and trim six or seven shelves.
Skills: Measuring and cutting, biscuit-joining, leveling, finding studs, attaching with screws.
Tools: Circular saw, level, drill, stud finder, nail set.

Customize ready-made shelves

Buy ready-made MDF shelving (see pages 82–83) ¾ inch thick and 10 inches wide. Finish with gloss or semigloss enamel for good looks and easy cleaning. Then give it a finished look by trimming the edges with a stained hardwood molding. Choose shelf brackets to suit your style.

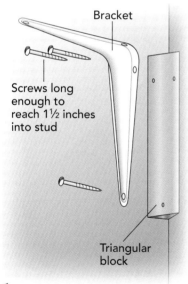

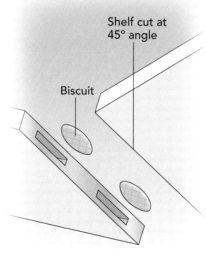

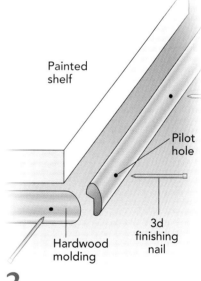

1. Attach the brackets.

Use a level to make horizontal pencil lines indicating the top of each shelf (so the lines will not be visible). Use a stud finder to locate studs and mark their locations. Install each bracket ¾ inch below the line, driving screws at least 1½ inches into studs. At the corner install a triangular block.

2. Install the shelves.

Cut the shelves to fit and set them on top of the brackets. If your wall is noticeably wavy, scribe a line along the wall at the back of the shelf using a pencil compass and cut with a jigsaw to fit against the wall. Paint the shelves. At corners, cut both pieces at 45-degree angles and join them with biscuits (see page 107).

3. Add the trim.

Stain the hardwood molding and apply polyurethane finish. Cut the molding with a mitersaw (see page 100). Make 45-degree miters at the corners. Install the molding by drilling pilot holes and driving in 3d finishing nails. Countersink the nails and fill the holes.

Making stackable shelves

These modules are easily moved and restacked. If you need to, you always can build more. Make modules of at least two heights—10 and 14 inches high are common dimensions—to accommodate your books. For yearbooks, magazines, and photo albums, you may need a module that is even taller. You will need one top piece for each tower of stackable shelves. Choose your lumber carefully: Twisted boards will not line up well. Use a hardwood such as oak and stain it, or build from pine and apply at least two coats of enamel paint.

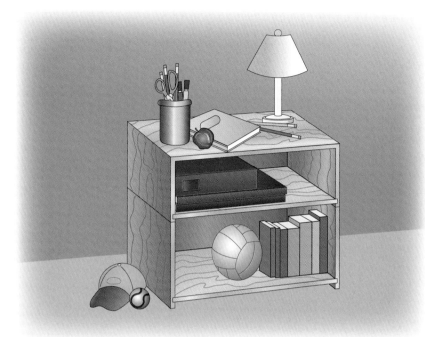

You'll Need

TIME: Three hours per module.
SKILLS: Measuring and marking, squaring, drilling straight holes, cutting dadoes and rabbets.
TOOLS: Circular saw, square, drill, dowel jig, hammer.

Versatile storage

If you build carefully, these units will fit together quite snugly. However, if you stack more than three, they may become unstable. If that happens, use angle brackets and screws to attach the top shelf to the wall.

Dowels and dadoes

Use 1×12 for the sides, shelves, and top. Cut the sidepieces to the height of the module (the usable interior height is ¾ inch less for stacked units, 1¾ inches less with the top installed). Cut the shelf to length (interior width is ¾ inch less than the shelf length). Cut a ¼×⅜-inch rabbet along the inside back edge of each sidepiece and the upper back edge of the shelf. Cut a ¾×⅜-inch dado located 1 inch up from the bottom of each sidepiece (see pages 108–111).

Attach the shelf in the dadoes, using wood glue and 4d finishing nails, checking for square. Cut a back out of ¼-inch plywood to fit into the rabbets and attach it with wood glue and 3d finishing nails.

Use a drill and dowel jig (see page 106) to drill holes in the top and bottom edges as shown. Also drill holes into the bottom of the top piece, being careful not to drill too deeply. Insert dowels (but don't glue them) as you stack the modules.

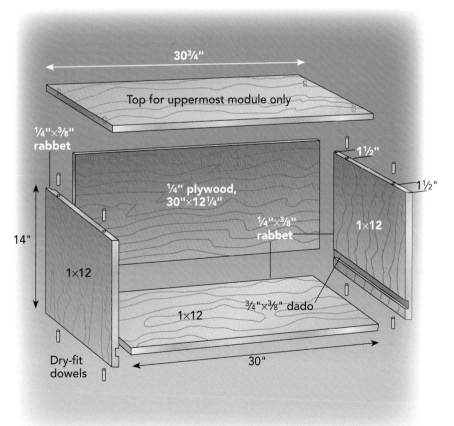

Building a basement wine rack

Most basements are cool and dark—ideal for storing wine. Here's a rack that stores your favorite vintages the right way: with the bottles on their sides.

Use the dark brown heartwood of redwood or cedar so it will not rot in damp conditions. Apply a sealer-preservative, paying special attention to the feet.

Although this unit has feet for stability, it is a good idea to anchor it to the wall or to joists.

You'll Need

TIME: Two or three days.
SKILLS: Measuring and cutting, cutting curves, cutting dadoes, attaching with screws.
TOOLS: Circular saw, jigsaw, drill, hole saw, square, level, clamp, chisel.

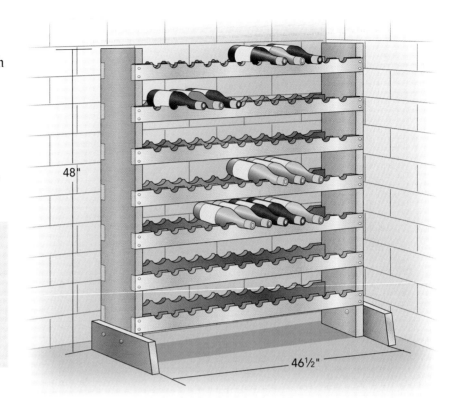

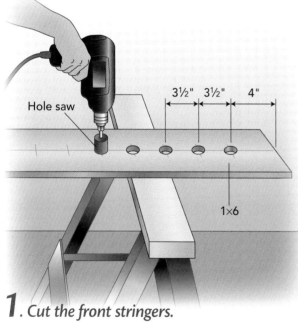

1. Cut the front stringers.

To make the two front stringers, draw a line lengthwise along the center of a 1×6. Mark the centerline 4 inches from one end, then every 3½ inches. The last mark should be 4 inches from the other end. Use a hole saw to cut a 1½-inch hole in the center of each mark. Rip-cut the board in half along the centerline.

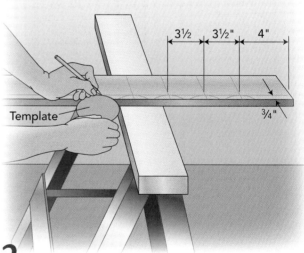

2. Lay out the rear stringers.

Rip another 1×6 in half and cut the pieces to the same length as the front stringers. On one of the boards, draw a line ¾ inch from the edge all along its length. Mark centerlines as you did in Step 1, first at 4 inches and then every 3½ inches. Cut a 4-inch circle from a piece of cardboard to use as a template and use it to mark for scallops as shown, with the bottom of the arcs at the intersections of the line and the marks.

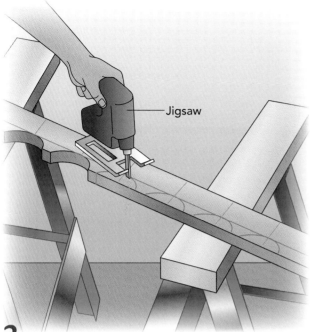

3. Cut the rear stringers.

Use a jigsaw to cut the scallops (see page 97). Work carefully and methodically to cut smooth curves. Make sure the blade is at an exact 90-degree angle to the saw base. Use the first piece as a template to mark for the other rear stringers and cut them the same way. Sand the cutouts smooth.

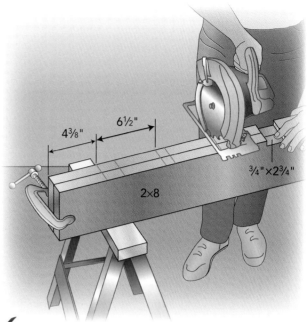

4. Notch and cut the standards.

Clamp two 2×8s together with their ends flush. Lay out notches the width of the stringers on one edge. Place the first notch 4⅜ inches from the bottom, then space them 6½ inches. Cut ¾-inch-deep notches on one edge of both boards, then flip the boards and cut notches at the same locations on the other edge. Chisel out the waste.

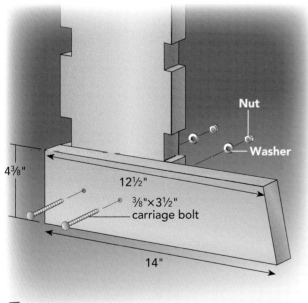

5. Attach the feet.

Cut the feet from 2×6 using the dimensions shown. Clamp a foot onto the bottom of one standard, with the bottom edges flush; drill holes, and attach with two ⅜×3½-inch carriage bolts. Repeat for the other foot.

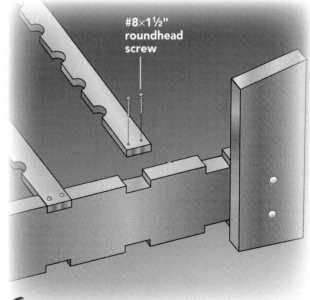

6. Attach the stringers.

Lay the standards on edge and set the front stringers in the notches. At each joint, drill two pilot holes and drive two 1½-inch #8 roundhead brass screws. Repeat for the rear stringers.

Chapter Four

Materials and Tools

Buying lumber for shelving and storage units is easy if you know a little about the materials available and consider the end use of your project. When you just need sturdy storage shelves for a garage, you can buy different materials than you would for living-room shelves.

This chapter begins with a look at lumber and sheet goods such as plywood. By understanding lumber grading and being familiar with common wood species, you'll be able to make smart choices when you go to the lumberyard or home center. In addition, there are tips on buying trim and moldings, storing lumber, and buying hardware.

TOOLS FOR THE JOB

Many of the projects in this book can be built with the most basic of tools—a hammer, handsaw, and screwdriver. In most cases, though, you'll achieve better results faster and with less effort by using some power tools.

The second part of this chapter shows a variety of tools, both hand and power, that will come in handy for storage and shelving projects. In many cases one tool can accomplish several jobs. A cordless drill/driver is one example: With it you can drive and remove screws as well as drill holes. It is almost indispensable for any homeowner or do-it-yourselfer.

Selecting lumber

Lumber for cabinets and shelves falls into two categories: boards and dimension lumber. Boards are nominally 1 inch thick (see chart, opposite page); dimension lumber, used for framing, is nominally 2 to 5 inches thick. Widths for both go up to 12 inches nominal. The lumber is originally cut to the nominal size, but milling reduces the size. Choose the highest-quality lumber you can afford for a project; good lumber makes the project go more smoothly. Even for painted utility shelves in a garage, choose each board very carefully, looking at each surface as well as sighting down its length. A slight **bow** or **crook** and some **twists** can be straightened as you fasten the board. A **cupped** board can be straightened only if you drive fasteners along its edges. A tight **knot** is only a cosmetic problem, but a loose knot may fall out. **Checking** is a surface problem, but a **split** cannot be repaired and will probably grow.

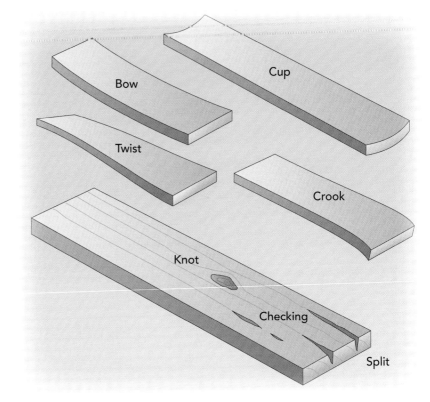

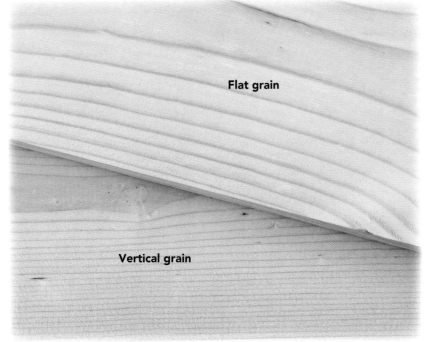

Vertical and flat grain

Depending on how a board is cut from the log, it will have vertical grain, with narrow, closely spaced grain lines, or flat grain, with wavy, widely spaced lines. Many boards are a combination of the two. Vertical-grain wood is stronger and less likely to warp than flat-grain wood. So choose boards with narrow grain lines whenever possible.

Common grades of lumber

Wood grading systems can vary depending on the species, the manufacturer, and even the lumberyard. Here are some common grades:

■ The best hardwood boards are graded "firsts" and "seconds" (FAS grade includes both). They are clear or nearly clear. "Select" boards have small knots on one side only. No. 1 and 2 common boards have more defects. For shelving that will be painted, or for a rustic look, use No. 2 common lumber.

■ The best softwoods are classified "select." Grade A select is clear, with no knots or blemishes. B, C, and D select have increasingly more and larger knots and blemishes.

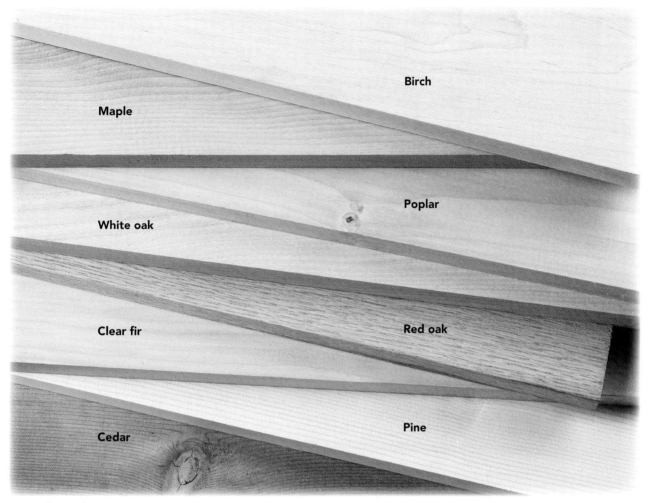

Maple

Birch

White oak

Poplar

Clear fir

Red oak

Cedar

Pine

Wood species

Hardwood comes from deciduous trees that grow slowly, making the lumber hard and durable and often very expensive. Although it is often available in standard sizes (see chart right), sometimes it is milled to odd widths to make use of as much wood as possible. Thicknesses may be stated in quarter inches—5/4, or five-quarter, boards start out $1\frac{1}{4}$ inches thick and are milled to about 1 inch thick. If the boards are smoothed on only two sides (S2S), the edges will be too rough and uneven to use, so have the yard saw or plane the edges.

Maple is extremely hard and difficult to cut. It is usually very light in color but can be reddish. **Red oak,** which is actually reddish brown, has a distinctive open grain; it resists warping but may shrink. **White oak's** grain is not quite so pronounced. It is lighter and more consistent in color than red oak and is more resistant to shrinking. **Birch** is similar in appearance and hardness to maple and it is less expensive.

Poplar is the lightest, softest, and least expensive of these hardwoods. The grain of poplar is not especially pretty, so it's a good choice for pieces that will be painted or for areas that will not be visible.

Softwood, which comes from coniferous trees, not only is softer but has a more casual appearance than hardwood. Use it for projects that will not receive much direct contact; even if painted, it can be easily dented.

Pine is very light and soft, making it easy to work with but weak. It resists warping but is prone to shrinkage. **Fir** is the strongest and heaviest of the softwoods listed here. Clear fir is hard, a good choice for outdoor furniture. **Cedar** is extremely soft, with a distinctive cream-to-brown color. Use aromatic red cedar for a pleasant smell and resistance to moth infestation.

MEASUREMENTS

Lumber sizes

A board that was 2 inches thick and 4 inches wide when cut is called a 2×4. But shrinkage and milling reduce the measurements to $1\frac{1}{2}$ inches by $3\frac{1}{2}$ inches when you buy it. "2×4" is the nominal size; the true dimensions are the actual size. Here are some common lumber sizes:

Nominal Size	Actual Size
1×2	$\frac{3}{4}"\times1\frac{1}{2}"$
1×4	$\frac{3}{4}"\times3\frac{1}{2}"$
1×6	$\frac{3}{4}"\times5\frac{1}{2}"$
1×8	$\frac{3}{4}"\times7\frac{1}{4}"$
1×10	$\frac{3}{4}"\times9\frac{1}{4}"$
1×12	$\frac{3}{4}"\times11\frac{1}{4}"$
2×2	$1\frac{1}{2}"\times1\frac{1}{2}"$
2×6	$1\frac{1}{2}"\times5\frac{1}{2}"$

Choosing sheet goods

You can create large surfaces easily and inexpensively with sheet goods. However, the edges will have to be covered, and the surface will rarely be good-looking enough to stain.

Plywood has great strength and resistance to cracking because it is made from layers of veneer with grains running in opposite directions. Softwood plywood is the most common, but you can buy sheets with veneers made of almost any kind of hardwood.

Hardboard is the least expensive of these sheet goods. Tempered hardboard is water-resistant, but will swell and weaken if soaked. Perforated hardboard with hooks is a quick shop storage option.

Particleboard is made of glued sawdust and very small chips, making it hard but easily broken. Use it as a substrate for laminate.

Medium-density fiberboard (MDF) uses even finer wood fiber to create a smooth and workable surface. It can be sanded smooth. Painted, it makes a serviceable and fairly strong finished surface. However, like particleboard, it can easily split when nails or screws are driven through it. Both of these products expand and weaken if they become wet. Plywood with medium-density fiberboard on one face (MDO, or medium-density overlay) gives a smooth face for painting.

Particleboard or MDF can be covered with **melamine,** a thin layer of plastic. Use melamine board for cabinet and shelf parts that will not get bumped much.

Wafer board is made of wood chips glued together in a random pattern. **Oriented strand board** (OSB) arranges the chips so they run in one direction for one layer, then at right angles for the next layer. OSB is nearly as strong as plywood. Both have rough surfaces and should be used only where they will not be visible, or for utility shelving.

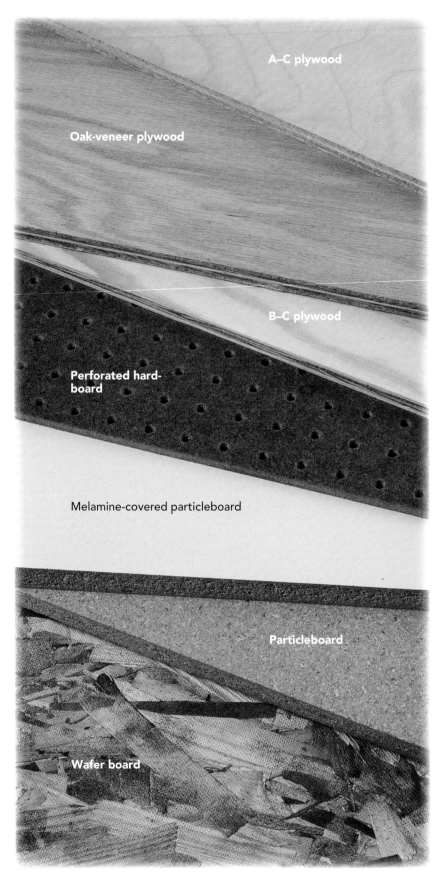

A–C plywood

Oak-veneer plywood

B–C plywood

Perforated hardboard

Melamine-covered particleboard

Particleboard

Wafer board

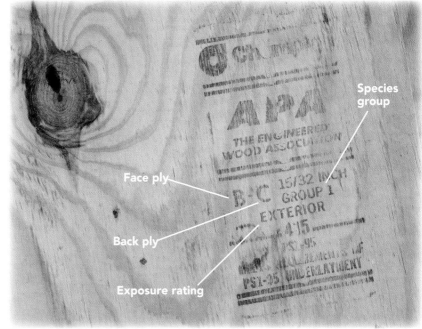

Plywood grading

The large letters on a softwood plywood grading stamp indicate the face grades. An "A" surface has no knots; a "B" face has only small, tight knots; "C" and "D" sides have progressively larger knots and rougher grain. This sheet has one "B" side and one "C" side. If the stamp says "Group 1," it uses a wood species rated the strongest; "Group 2" is less strong. An "exterior" rating means that it will resist moisture well.

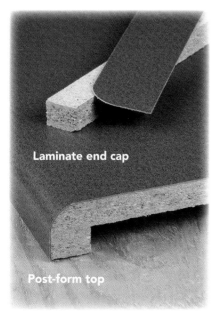

Laminated countertop

Countertops usually have a sheet of hard plastic laminated to particleboard. You can make your own square-edged top by attaching plastic laminate to particleboard with contact cement. A post-form top has rounded edges and must be factory-made.

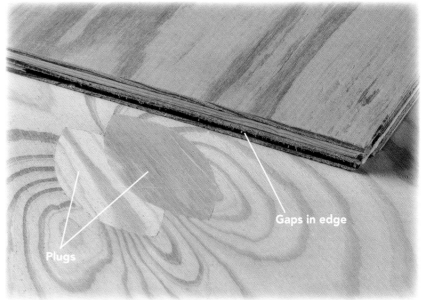

Plywood defects

A plywood face is rarely perfect, but surfaces for better grades are repaired more skillfully. The best surfaces use small pieces of repair wood that match the surrounding area so they are barely noticed. Lower-grade surfaces use large plugs, sometimes in the shape of footballs and often clearly different from their surroundings. If you are going to paint, make sure that the patch feels smooth.

Gaps along the edge should be filled with wood filler or else the edge will be easily damaged. If an area feels softer than the surrounding area, it is hollow.

Selecting moldings

Nothing spruces up a plain piece of cabinetry quicker than a piece of molding. Home centers have a large selection of profiles to choose from. Most are designed for a specific purpose—baseboard for the bottom of a wall, casing for around doors, and so on. But you can use them any way you want. By stacking moldings, or positioning them next to each other, you can create a custom look.

Standard profile moldings are available in random lengths ranging from 4 to 20 feet. Whenever possible, order pieces long enough to span the entire distance; joints are almost always noticeable.

It is worth your while to measure for each piece and make a list. Buy only the sizes you need, adding a few inches extra for each piece.

Carved and embossed moldings come in standard lengths. Often they are worth the steep price, because a few pieces can have a dramatic effect on your project.

Pine molding is the most common. If you will be painting, primed molding—perhaps made of MDF (see page 82)—may be cheaper and will be easier to paint. Oak molding can lend a classy look: Make sure the grain and color match the wood it will abut. Paper-covered molding does not cut cleanly, making it difficult to work with. Plastic moldings cut easily and resist splitting. Many attractive profiles are made in plastic, including large crown moldings.

It may be difficult to find a factory piece to match the profile of an older molding. However, some lumberyards or wood shops will custom-mill molding for you. It may be worth the extra cost and trouble to get just the molding you want.

You can use a router to form a molding profile on a piece of wood. There is a wide variety of router bits; these can be set at various depths and used in combination to make unique edge profiles.

Finger-jointed molding

These inexpensive moldings use short pieces joined together end-to-end. As long as the joints are smooth (feel them to be sure), they will paint as well as standard molding; however, the finger joint will show through stain.

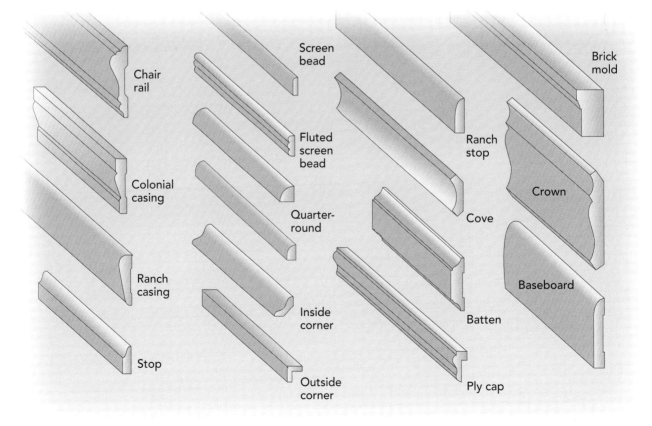

Chair rail

Colonial casing

Ranch casing

Stop

Screen bead

Fluted screen bead

Quarter-round

Inside corner

Outside corner

Ranch stop

Cove

Batten

Ply cap

Brick mold

Crown

Baseboard

Storing lumber

Trees are rarely straight, so it is in the nature of wood to twist. That is why even the best lumber will warp eventually if it is not stacked properly. And don't be surprised if a lower-grade board warps in a day or two.

Boards in the best lumberyards are always laid flat and stacked tightly against each other. You'll see lots of S-shaped pieces when boards or moldings are stored upright.

Plan a wood storage area for your home that can accommodate boards and sheets of various sizes and puts them within easy reach. Humidity causes warping, so store lumber in a cool, dry place if possible. Keep all wood off bare concrete floors, especially if there is the possibility of occasional flooding.

The best way to store sheet goods is to lay them flat. However, this takes up space and makes it difficult to get at the sheet on the bottom of the pile, so set them on edge. To minimize bowing, stand the sheets as close to upright as possible. Place narrower pieces on the outside of the stack.

Store long boards close to eye level so you can see each board's dimension by looking at the end. Use several racks so you don't have tall stacks of boards. You could assign one rack to molding, one to boards 1×4 and smaller, and one to wider boards.

Small pieces often come in handy when building cabinets. So set aside space for a variety of lengths and widths in your storage area. Provide a place for 4-foot-tall cutoffs from sheet goods. Also have several shelves for boards that are 4 feet or shorter in length.

When you stack the lumber, push all the pieces tightly against each other. Place the widest boards at the bottom and stack progressively narrower boards on them.

Sometimes correct storage can straighten a warped board. Set it on a flat surface, stack a board of the same size or larger on top of it, and place weights on top of both. In a month or so you should have a straight board.

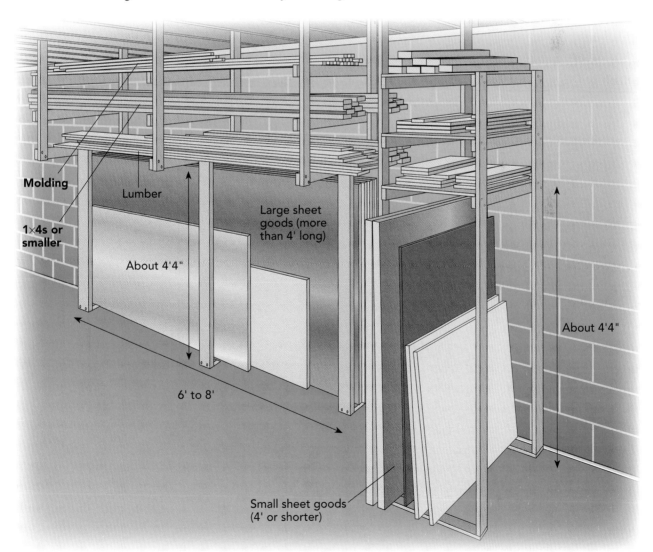

Molding

Lumber

1×4s or smaller

About 4'4"

Large sheet goods (more than 4' long)

6' to 8'

About 4'4"

Small sheet goods (4' or shorter)

Choosing fasteners and hardware

For most cabinetwork use **finishing** nails or **trim head** screws. Use a **casing** nail if the head will be exposed to moisture, a **wire brad** when attaching thin moldings. **Corrugated fasteners** work only as temporary fasteners. To build heavy framework, **cement-coated box** nails hold better than plain **common** or **box** nails. **Galvanized** nails resist rust and are good for outdoor projects. **Drywall** nails have ringed shanks to hold better. **Drywall** screws are called "all-purpose" because they are used for fastening most interior projects. A **flathead** screw is driven flush with the surface; **ovalhead** and **roundhead** screws protrude. For finish work, combine a flathead screw with a **trim washer.** Use **masonry** screws when attaching frames to concrete or brick. For the strongest joints, drill holes and install **bolts** or **lag** screws. **Hanger** screws are good for hanging fixtures from ceiling framing.

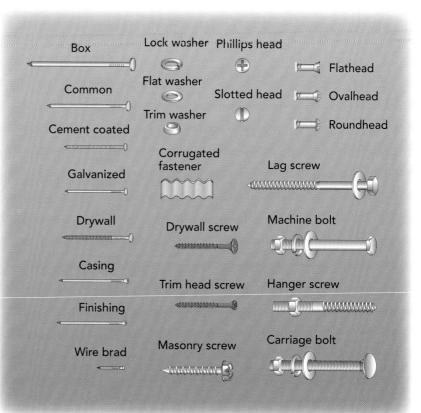

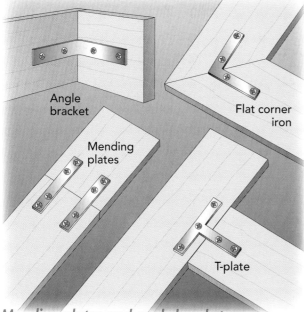

Mending plates and angle brackets

Use these only for areas that will not be visible. They provide a quick way to reinforce joints but should not be the only joint connectors. Clamp the boards together while you fasten. Drill a pilot hole and fasten one screw so it holds the metal piece in place. Then drill the rest of the pilot holes and drive those screws.

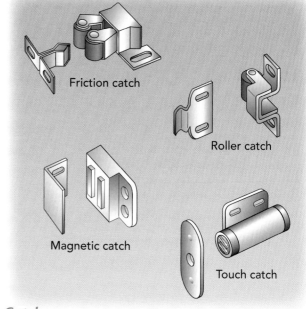

Catches

Each type of catch has a different feel, so choose one type and use it for all the cabinets in one area. If used constantly, catches may need to be replaced after about five years. **Friction** and **roller** catches are quiet and inexpensive but are the least durable. **Magnetic** catches close with a click. **Touch** catches are also magnetic and make pulls unnecessary.

Choose cabinet hardware.

Before choosing a hinge type, decide whether your cabinet will have flush or overlapped doors and whether the cabinet will be framed or frameless. Most cabinet doors are overlapped: They are larger than the opening and so overlap the cabinet opening by a fraction of an inch all around. This makes them easier to build and install than flush doors, which sit inside the opening and must fit perfectly to ensure an even gap between door and cabinet. Lipped doors have rabbeted edges that overlap the opening. Framed cabinets use vertical and horizontal pieces, usually of 1×2 or 1×3, to provide rigidity. Frameless cabinets are sleeker in appearance and must use **Euro-style** or **wraparound** hinges. Doors can slide in a **sliding track** instead of hanging on hinges.

The most common types of hinges are shown at right. (A bird's-eye view shows how they attach.) For a framed cabinet, the simplest configuration is an overlapped door and **semiconcealed** hinge. Square-cut the door to an inch larger than the opening, attach the hinges to the door, position the door, and attach the hinges to the frame. Lipped doors require **offset hinges.** To make sure they fit, buy the hinges before you cut the rabbet. For a flush door, use a **butt** hinge, a smaller version of the hinges used on household doors. **Pivot** hinges attach at the top and bottom of the door. A **concealed** hinge can't be seen when the door is closed.

Frameless cabinets use **Euro-style** hinges that fit into holes in both the door and cabinet. They are easy to install using a Forstner bit, which bores a very clean hole. These hinges have a big advantage: You can adjust them with a screwdriver to align all your doors after installation. Adjusting the other hinges requires moving screws over—a more difficult task.

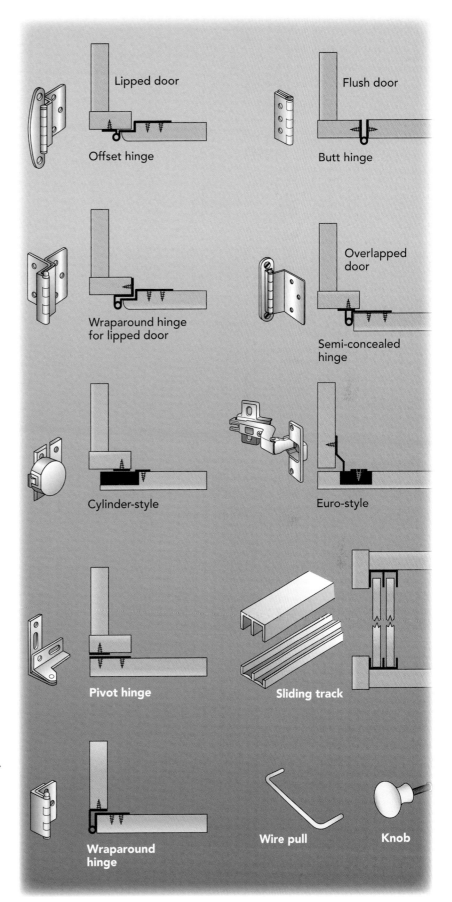

Lipped door
Offset hinge

Flush door
Butt hinge

Wraparound hinge for lipped door

Overlapped door
Semi-concealed hinge

Cylinder-style

Euro-style

Pivot hinge

Sliding track

Wraparound hinge

Wire pull

Knob

Choosing hand tools

Accurate, sharp, and comfortable tools make working with wood a pleasure; shoddy or ill-maintained tools turn it into a tiresome chore. Hand tools are less expensive than power tools, so don't hesitate to buy a hand tool when a project calls for it.

Keep your tools where you can find them easily and where they won't be damaged. If you have a shop, hang tools on hooks on perforated hardboard to keep them safe and handy. An inexpensive nylon-fabric insert for a 5-gallon bucket is a great way to haul hand tools. A leather tool pouch will make you feel like a real carpenter and puts the most-used tools within easy reach: knife, tape measure, chalkline, layout square, hammer, chisel, nail set, and screwdriver. Make a habit of putting these tools in the same holsters and you'll be quick on the draw.

A 25-foot **tape measure** with a 1-inch-wide blade will handle most measuring jobs. (The hook at its end slides back and forth the same distance as its thickness to give an accurate measurement whether you hook it on the end of a board or butt it up against a surface.)

With a **chalkline** you can make perfectly straight lines over long distances. Have plenty of **pencils** on hand; they have a habit of getting lost. A triangular **layout square** is sturdy, so it is easy to use as a guide for square circular-saw cuts and is not easily knocked out of alignment. Use a **T-bevel** to transfer odd angles. For checking large objects for square, or for drawing long square lines, a **framing square** (carpenter's square) is indispensable. Buy a **level** to check for plumb. An **awl** is handy for scribing layout lines and marking centers for drilling holes.

A **backsaw with miter box** enables you to make accurate square and 45-degree cuts in moldings and small boards. A **coping saw** is necessary to make coped cuts in molding (see page 100). Use a **drywall saw** or **keyhole saw** to make rough cuts in walls or boards, which are sometimes needed when installing cabinets. Have a **caulking gun** ready for applying adhesive.

Shave a board smoothly with an accurately adjusted **plane** that has a sharp blade. Sandpaper on a sanding block will complete the job. A **Surform tool** (rasping plane) takes less skill to use but produces a rough surface. Use a **rasp** to shape small areas. A **utility knife** comes in handy for trimming splinters and rough ends and for making precise measuring marks. Buy one with a retractable blade or reserve a pocket in your leather pouch for a knife with a fixed blade. **Chisels** are needed for mortising; have at least two sizes—½ inch and 1 inch.

You will need **phillips-head** and **slot-head screwdrivers**—at least two sizes of each. A combination screwdriver has four tips and is easier to keep track of than four screwdrivers. Use an **awl** to make starter holes for small screws.

Tongue-and-groove pliers grip objects of various sizes and give you plenty of leverage. **Locking pliers** keep a tight grip while you work with two hands. Use an **adjustable (crescent) wrench** to tighten and loosen bolts and nuts. A good selection of **clamps** (see pages 104–105) will enable you to firmly glue together many cabinet projects and damaged furniture.

You'll use your **hammer** often, so choose one that is comfortable. A 16-ounce one with curved claws is the most popular choice, but a 22-ounce hammer drives large nails faster. Buy variously sized **nail sets** so you can set and countersink small and large finish nails. A **pry bar** is indispensable for demolition.

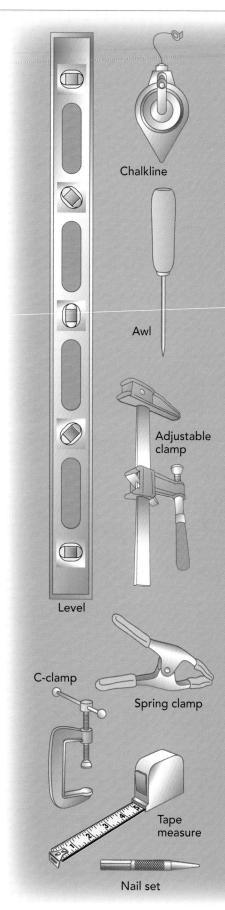

Chalkline

Awl

Level

Adjustable clamp

C-clamp

Spring clamp

Tape measure

Nail set

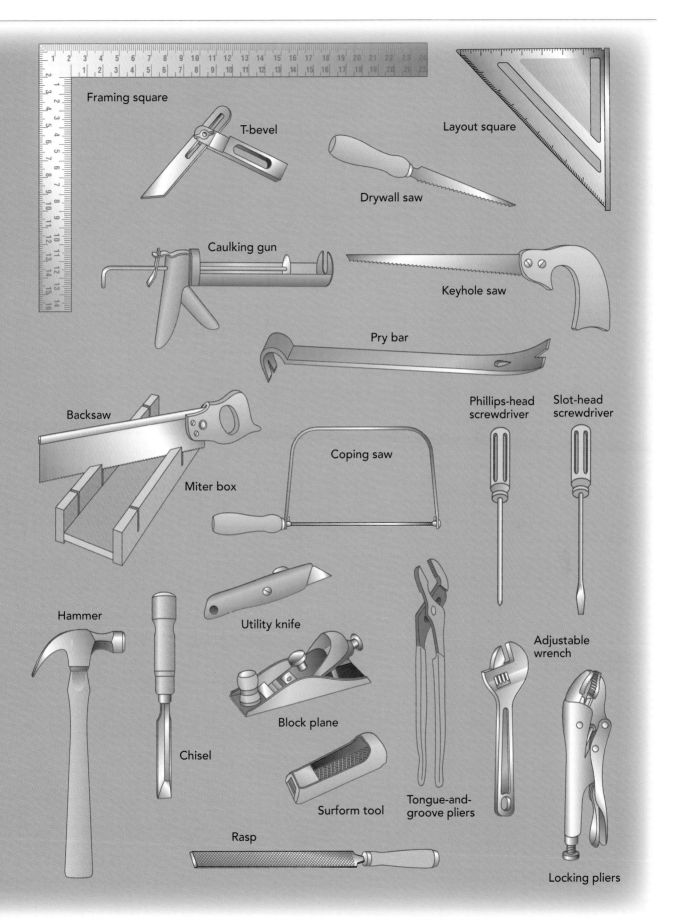

Framing square

T-bevel

Layout square

Drywall saw

Caulking gun

Keyhole saw

Pry bar

Backsaw

Coping saw

Miter box

Phillips-head screwdriver

Slot-head screwdriver

Hammer

Utility knife

Adjustable wrench

Block plane

Chisel

Surform tool

Tongue-and-groove pliers

Rasp

Locking pliers

Selecting power tools

You can make shelves and straightforward cabinets using the same tools you need for house repairs and remodeling. The basic trio of circular saw, drill, and jigsaw will equip you to cut most any line, bore any hole, and drive screws.

For all the tools shown on these two pages, amperage rather than horsepower is an indication of power. A tool with ball bearings will make work more pleasant.

A carpenter uses a **circular saw** constantly. It crosscuts, rips boards lengthwise, and makes miter and beveled cuts. A high-quality circular saw used with a guide will make good cuts. When shopping, look for a saw rated at 12 amps or more and that uses ball bearings—

a combination that will make for smooth cuts and long life. When you turn on the motor, it should run smoothly and there should be absolutely no wobble in the blade. The baseplate should be rigid and easy to adjust. A saw with a 7¼-inch blade is a good all-purpose tool. For cabinetwork, consider buying a smaller, lighter model. Use a hollow-ground planer blade or a plywood blade when you need precise cuts.

A variable-speed, reversible **electric drill** with a ⅜-inch chuck is essential for carpenter and woodworker alike. It should draw at least 3.5 amps. A keyless chuck allows you to change bits very quickly, but it's hard for some

people to adequately tighten the bits. Buy a drill with a keyed chuck if you can't tighten the keyless one.

A **cordless drill/driver** is the best tool for driving screws, and you can use it for drilling too. Buy at least a 12-volt model. A second battery pack is a must-have.

Maintain a complete selection of twist drills, from 1/16 to ⅜ inch in diameter. Brad-point bits cut cleaner holes than standard twist bits. For larger holes use inexpensive spade bits, hole saws, or, for the cleanest cuts, Forstner bits.

Choose a **jigsaw** that draws at least 3 amps. The baseplate should be rigid and the angle-adjusting mechanism easy to use. It should be possible to tighten the baseplate

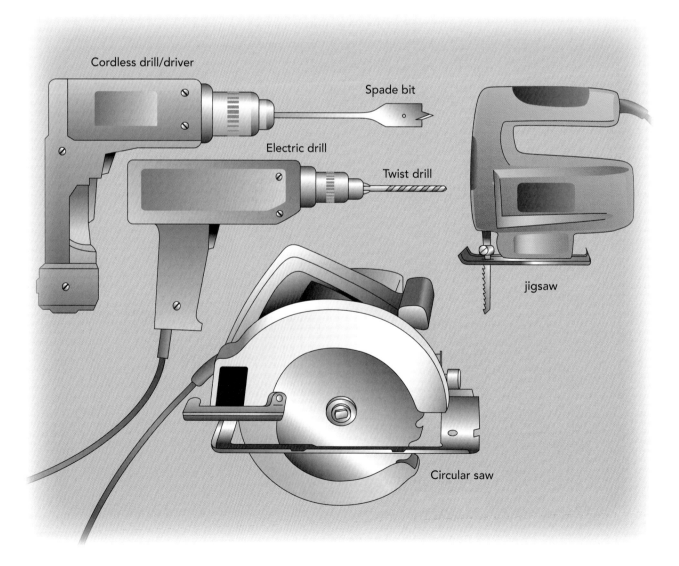

Cordless drill/driver

Spade bit

Electric drill

Twist drill

jigsaw

Circular saw

securely in any position. Variable speed gives you more control over your cuts. A scrolling knob allows you to make turns without having to get into awkward positions.

Some tools are not used often but are essential on occasion. If you seldom use them, you can buy a less expensive tool or rent a professional-quality tool.

A **router** allows you to mill lumber edges to almost any shape; a vast variety of router bits is available (see page 101). The best way to get clean, even cuts is to set the router in a router table. Guides can be nearly as accurate. A self-piloted bit, with a roller that runs along the edge it is cutting, can make straight cuts, but only if the edge it is rolling against is straight.

With a **biscuit joiner,** you can quickly join pieces edge to edge with the faces of the pieces perfectly flush with each other. You can also join pieces face to edge. You will need to glue and clamp the pieces (see pages 106–107).

A **power mitersaw,** often called a chop saw or cutoff saw, easily makes accurate crosscuts and simple miter cuts. A model using a 10-inch blade will miter-cut boards up to 2×6. A compound mitersaw costs more but is more versatile. If you anticipate projects calling for compound miter cuts, such as installing crown molding, the compound saw is essential. A thin-kerf carbide-tipped blade with at least 40 teeth will cut cleanly and last a long time.

A **belt sander** will quickly remove material from a large area. It should be fairly heavy and have a dust collector. Check that it uses a belt size that is commonly available: 3×24 and 3×21 inches are popular.

Maintain a selection of belts of at least three grits. If you have belts of 50, 80, and 120 grit, you will be able to both remove material quickly and bring a surface to a fairly smooth finish. A belt sander has definite limitations, however. Unless used carefully, it can quickly dig surprisingly deep gouges in wood. Use the belt sander for rough work, and finish-sand by hand or use a vibrating or random-orbit sander.

A **random-orbit sander** works by moving in small random circles, rather than just vibrating. It removes material more quickly than an older vibrating sander, but some people feel the resulting finish is not as smooth. If you need to sand in tight spots, a detail sander is a good investment. Have a variety of sandpapers on hand ranging from 80 grit to 320 grit.

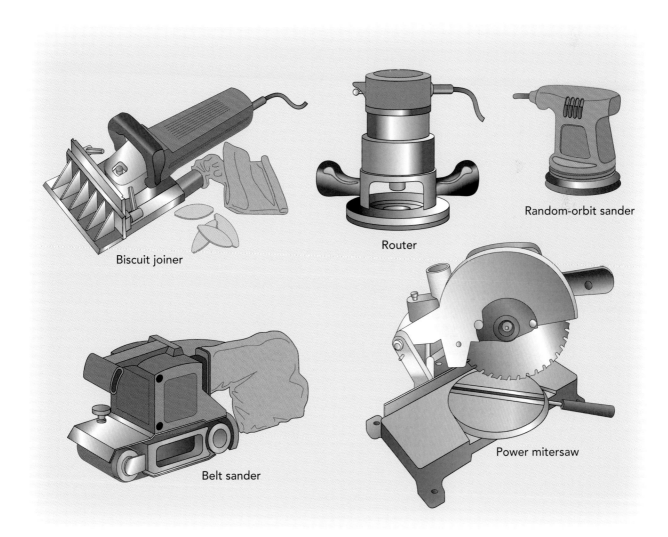

Biscuit joiner

Router

Random-orbit sander

Belt sander

Power mitersaw

Choosing shop tools

A well-equipped shop is a must for a serious cabinetmaker. It need not be large or elaborate; but without a well-organized, brightly lit, and comfortable place to work, building will be a struggle and results may be disappointing.

■ The first thing you need is a work surface. It must be flat and even and large enough to hold your projects; otherwise, it will be hard to build things that are square in both directions. You could work on the floor, but that will get tiresome in a hurry as you will be on your knees. A simple 8-foot by 3-foot workbench, 40 inches tall and made of ¾-inch plywood and 2×4s, makes a fine worktable.

■ Place stationary power tools so that you can easily position wood on them. For a tablesaw or radial-arm saw, you must be able to slide full 4×8 sheets of plywood all the way through. Position your workbench or other supporting structure so that the plywood sheets have a surface to rest on.

■ Provide plenty of light, directed so your body won't make shadows while you work. Large fluorescent fixtures work best.

■ Place 20-amp electrical receptacles in convenient places so you won't have a tangle of extension cords. For a shop with several power tools, consider putting in a separate circuit.

■ Make it easy to clean your shop—and to keep dust from filtering into the rest of the house. Place a large garbage can where you can toss scraps of wood right after cutting. Use dust bags on power tools whenever possible. Keep a workshop vac plugged in and within easy reach. An exhaust fan—even a box fan placed in a window—will blow fine dust out of the room. The best and most expensive solution is a central dust collector with tubes running to all the power tools.

■ Keep your hand tools in sight and within easy reach. A sheet of perforated hardboard attached to 1×2 furring strips on the wall is a time-tested method. If tool hooks pop out too easily, glue them in place with construction adhesive.

■ Provide storage for lumber (see pages 32 and 85) and for fasteners and other hardware. Store nails and screws on shelves. Use labels to mark their sizes so you don't have to dig through them to find the screw you want.

Consider attaching jar lids to an overhead surface (page 33) so that you can unscrew a glass jar full of nails or screws with one hand.

A **tablesaw** (see pages 98–99 and 110–111) can handle most cutting and grooving jobs and will be in use frequently. In fact, you may want to design your entire shop around it; it will be the workhorse of your shop.

Choose a tablesaw with a solid table that will not vibrate while

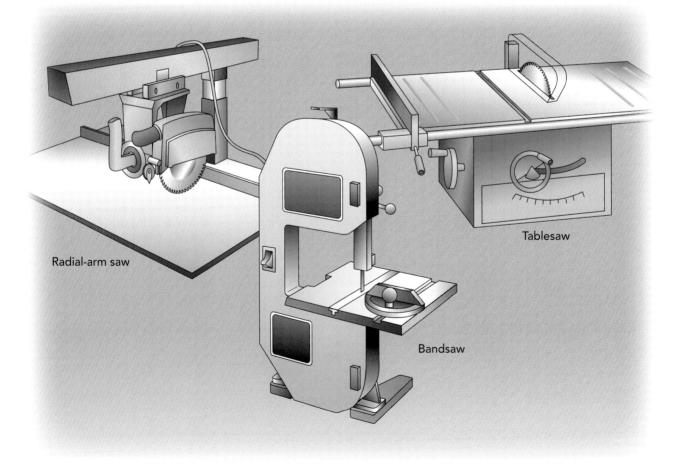

Radial-arm saw

Bandsaw

Tablesaw

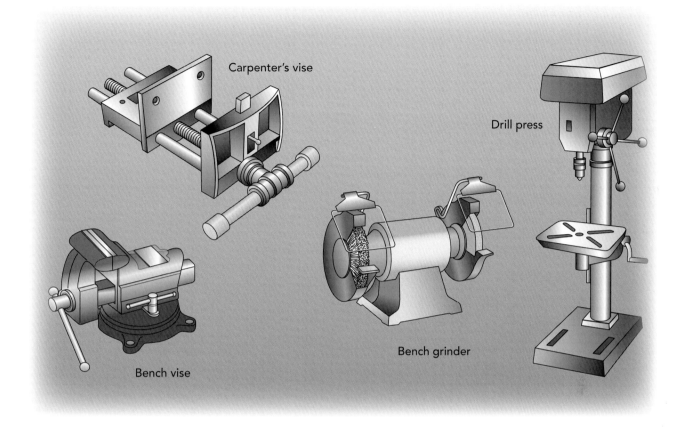

Carpenter's vise

Drill press

Bench grinder

Bench vise

you work. The rip fence is very important. It should stay firmly in place when clamped, align perfectly parallel to the blade, and be easy to move. The miter guide should slide smoothly and easily in its grooves.

The more powerful the motor, the better. A belt-driven model works more smoothly and lasts longer than one that has the blade attached directly to the motor.

Some portable (or benchtop) tablesaws can make accurate cuts, but a freestanding contractor's or cabinet saw will be worth the extra price in the long run. The most popular size that woodworkers use is a 10-inch blade. If you pay the extra money for a carbide-tipped combination blade with 40 or more teeth, you will be able to make splinter-free cuts for a long time before changing blades.

A 10-inch **radial-arm** saw is also an all-purpose tool, though you will find making long rip cuts

easier with a tablesaw. Unless you buy the best quality model, its cuts will probably be slightly less precise than those made by a good tablesaw. Make sure the motor glides easily and without wobbling during crosscuts. When clamped in position for a rip cut, it should be unshakable. The crank for raising and lowering the blade should operate easily. Instead of a radial-arm saw, many woodworkers prefer the combination of a tablesaw and compound mitersaw.

Use a **bandsaw** to make straight or curved cuts. You will sometimes be limited in making curved cuts; the throat size limits the capacity. A heavy-duty model can rip-cut or crosscut like a tablesaw. To make inside cuts, as for scrollwork, use a **scrollsaw** or **jigsaw.**

You can bore accurate holes using a jig and a standard hand drill (see page 106), but a **drill press** makes it much easier. The table should tilt,

for drilling at angles. See that the motor and bit move up and down without the slightest wobble and that the table can be adjusted easily and clamped firmly in position.

A **bench grinder** is an inexpensive tool that also can be surprisingly handy. Use it to sharpen chisels and plane blades as well as for a variety of household sharpening chores.

A standard **bench vise** is mounted with lag screws or bolts on top of the workbench and is useful for holding a variety of objects. However, a **carpenter's vise** is better for most woodworking projects. It mounts to the side of the bench, and the wider jaws grip boards without denting them. (To make it even less likely to dent boards, attach pieces of wood to the inside of the jaws.)

Chapter Five

Basic Skills

Every carpentry or woodworking project requires fundamental skills such as measuring, cutting, and joining. This chapter shows a number of techniques and skills that will ensure success in building your storage and shelving projects.

Here you will learn how to make accurate cuts and strong joints and how to use specialty tools such as the router and biscuit joiner. Many handy tips and tricks are included that will make your work go faster and easier. From cutting with a circular saw to applying a finish, all the skills you need to complete the projects in this book are shown in this chapter. You can also rely on it as a reference for future home improvement projects.

Using a circular saw or jigsaw

Begin cutting with a circular saw or jigsaw by placing the front of the baseplate on the board, keeping the blade back from the board. Pull the trigger and allow the motor to reach full speed, then push the blade into the cut. Focus your eyes on the blade as you cut, not the notch. Find the correct path and push through with a smooth stroke. Don't make small changes in direction as you cut. Before using your circular saw to make precise cuts with a guide, learn to use it as a general carpentry tool. Take some time to practice: Draw a series of square lines across a board and slice through them one by one. Once you feel comfortable and can cut straight lines by hand, you'll be better prepared to use a guide. With a jigsaw make practice cuts until you can make both smooth curves and even straight cuts. Your first tries will no doubt go astray; practice until you get the knack.

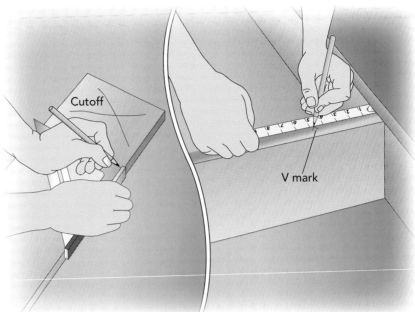

Measure and mark

To pinpoint the cutoff spot, draw a V instead of a straight line to show your measurement; the tip marks the exact spot. To make the cutoff line, hold the tip of the pencil on the tip of the V and slide the layout square over to it. Draw the line, then mark an X where the waste will be so that you can be sure to cut on the correct side of the line. When possible, hold a board in position to mark its length rather than using a tape measure.

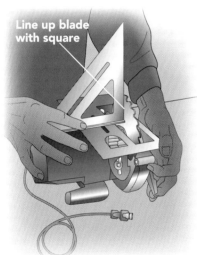

Square the blade

Before cutting make sure that your blade is square; the guide on the saw may be inaccurate. Hold a layout square against the blade. To test, crosscut a 2×4. Flip one side over; if the cut edges meet perfectly, the blade is square.

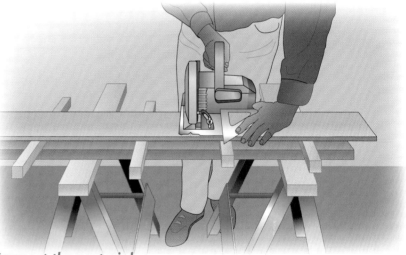

Support the material

A board that is not properly supported can bind the blade, causing the saw to kick back dangerously. If the scrap piece is short, support the board on the good side and let the scrap fall. Letting a longer scrap fall will produce splinters or cause binding, so support the board in four places. Make sure the two inner supports are not lower than the outer supports, or the board will bow downward and bind. You can cut the board roughly to size, then make the finish cut.

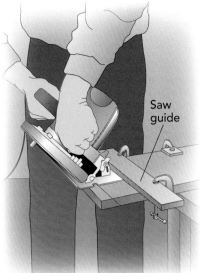

Bevel cut

Circular saw bevel guides are often not reliable, so test on a scrap before making a cut. You can use a layout square or a T-bevel to check the blade. You may need to retract the blade guard—it could cause the cut to go astray. This is a difficult cut, so brace the board and clamp a guide onto it.

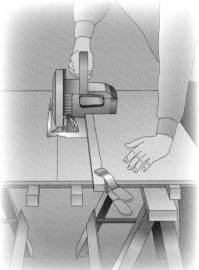

Long cut in sheet goods

Support the sheet in four places so that after the cut is made, the two pieces will be stable. Measure the distance between the outside of the baseplate and the blade—keeping in mind which side of the line you want to cut—and clamp a straightedge as a guide. Don't press too hard against the guide.

Score across grain or veneer.

To make sure you do not produce splinters when cutting a veneer or cutting across the grain, use a knife and straightedge to score a line that is about $1/16$ inch above the cutline. When cutting a door or other object with a thin veneer, knife-cut all the way through the veneer—it may take several passes.

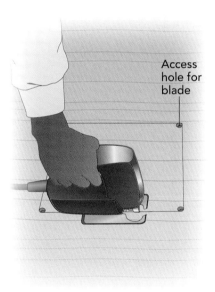

Inside cut with jigsaw

When cutting out an area on the inside of a board, first bore at least one hole, large enough for the jigsaw blade to fit in, inside the cutlines. When you cut with a jigsaw, it is important to keep the baseplate flat on the board. Press down on the board with more pressure than you use for pushing forward.

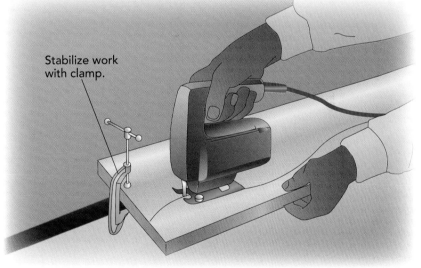

Curved cuts

To cut a long curve, make sure that the board is clamped tightly and that there are no obstructions to the cut under the board. Make sure that the baseplate thumbscrew is firmly tightened; wobbling is the most common cause of ugly jigsaw cuts.

With practice you can make cuts that are evenly arced. The trick is to turn the saw with steady consistency as you push forward at a constant speed. This produces a smoother cut than making frequent small turns and corrections.

Move slowly without forcing the blade. Avoid sharp turns—that can easily break a blade. If you wander from the line, back up and try again. If the saw heats up or if you smell smoke, stop.

Cutting with a tablesaw and radial-arm saw

The best way to ensure accurate tablesaw and radial-arm saw cuts is to set up carefully. Make sure the blade is precisely square or tilted correctly. See that the tablesaw fence is perfectly parallel to the blade and that the miter gauge is at a perfect right angle or miter angle. Make test cuts on scrap lumber before you cut the real thing.

CAUTION!
Saw safety

Both tablesaws and radial-arm saws can be dangerous; even professionals can be injured. Never wear long sleeves or loose clothing. Keep fingers well away from the blade and use a push stick to keep your fingers away from the blade. Unplug the saw before making adjustments.

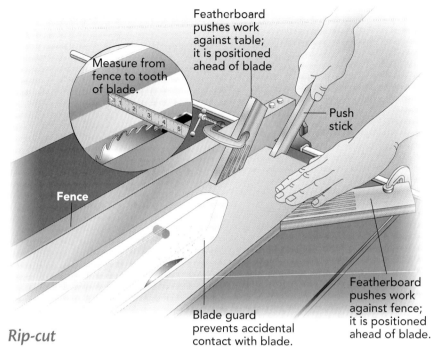

Featherboard pushes work against table; it is positioned ahead of blade

Push stick

Measure from fence to tooth of blade.

Fence

Blade guard prevents accidental contact with blade.

Featherboard pushes work against fence; it is positioned ahead of blade.

Rip-cut

Measure from the rip fence to the teeth of the blade. To be sure your cut will be accurate, make a cut in a scrap piece and measure it. Adjust the blade to ¼ inch above the top of the board. Start the motor and allow it to reach full speed. Hold the board so it glides smoothly and is tight against the fence at all points as you push it forward. Avoid stopping and starting as much as possible; that can make the cut irregular.

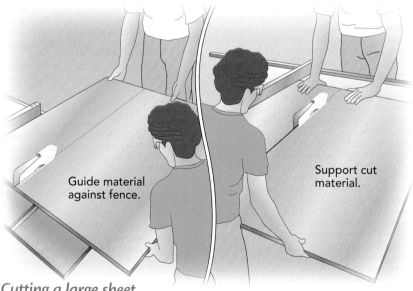

Guide material against fence.

Support cut material.

Cutting a large sheet.

With practice and a good worktable beyond the saw, you can learn to cut full sheets by yourself. But it is safer to have a helper stand to the side to assist you in positioning the sheet up against the fence. Turn on the saw and push the sheet through, all the time making sure it is against the fence. Halfway through the cut the helper should move behind the saw to support the portion of the sheet leaving the table.

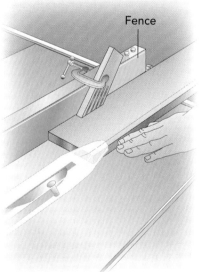

Fence

Beveled rip-cut

It may be hard to get this aligned. After adjusting the bevel, hold the board against the rip fence and slide both of them until the blade lines up with the cutline. Make a small test cut first.

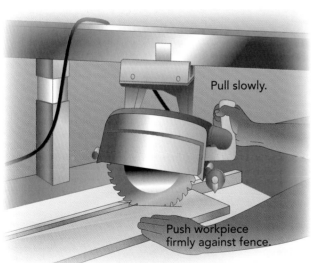

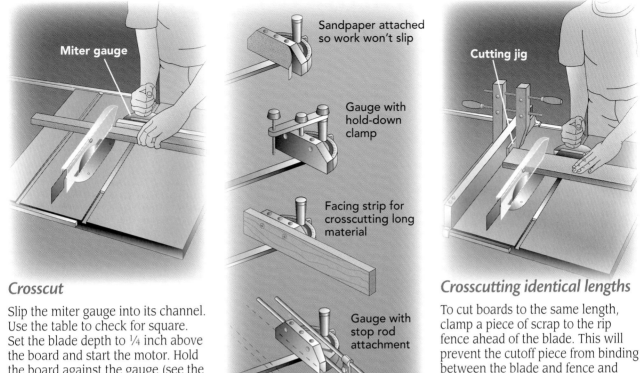

Crosscut

Slip the miter gauge into its channel. Use the table to check for square. Set the blade depth to ¼ inch above the board and start the motor. Hold the board against the gauge (see the helpers at right) and slide it through the blade. Hold the board only on the gauge side of the blade; it will bind if you hold both sides.

Sandpaper attached so work won't slip

Gauge with hold-down clamp

Facing strip for crosscutting long material

Gauge with stop rod attachment

Crosscutting identical lengths

To cut boards to the same length, clamp a piece of scrap to the rip fence ahead of the blade. This will prevent the cutoff piece from binding between the blade and fence and being kicked back. Measure the length from the blade to the face of the scrap. Hold the workpiece firmly as you slide it off the jig to cut it.

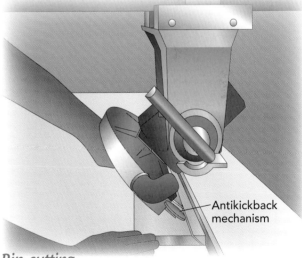

Pull slowly.

Push workpiece firmly against fence.

Antikickback mechanism

Crosscut or miter-cut with a radial-arm saw

There is a tightening lever that must be loosened every time you change from crosscut to rip-cut. If you don't tighten it again before making a cut, the blade will wobble. See that the board lies perfectly flat on the table. With the saw running, lower the blade so it cuts just below the surface. Hold the board flush against the fence and pull slowly to make sure the blade hits the cutline exactly. Then pull the saw through in one motion. Pull slowly, especially if cutting 2× lumber or hardwood; if you pull too fast, the saw will bind.

Rip-cutting

For rip-cutting, the blade rotates up against the board—the opposite of a crosscut. For a beveled rip like the one shown, you will need to raise the blade as much as several inches before it can be positioned for the bevel. Start the motor with the blade slightly above the table, then lower it. Position the antikickback mechanism so it will grab the board if it starts to shoot backward. If the motor stops midcut, shut it off immediately, pull the board back, and start again. If the motor overheats and turns itself off, wait a few minutes before you push the reset button.

Cutting molding

A miter joint is made of two pieces that are angle-cut or bevel-cut at the same angle and then joined together. Most often two pieces cut to 45 degrees are joined to make a 90-degree corner. If miter cuts are off even half a degree, the joint will look sloppy.

An inexpensive plastic or wood miter box like the one at right can make accurate cuts, but you'll need to struggle a bit to achieve real precision. Another type of miter box uses what looks like a hacksaw running through a sliding mechanism; it will be more precise and easier to use. The easiest way to cut molding is with a power mitersaw (page 91).

Most mistakes occur not in the cutting but in the measuring. When possible make the miter cut first and hold the piece in its final position so you can mark for the straight cut at the other end. It's easy to get confused about the direction of the miter cut; hold the piece in place to be sure.

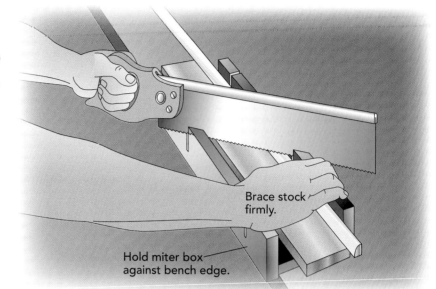

Brace stock firmly.

Hold miter box against bench edge.

Miter-cutting by hand

With a box like this one, place a scrap of 1×4 in the bottom so you can saw completely through the piece without cutting through the bottom of the miter box. To avoid confusion place the board or molding in the position it will be when in use. Firmly push the piece up against the far side of the miter box. Start the cut slowly to make sure you are cutting on the right side of the line. Hold the piece tightly as you saw, or it may pop out.

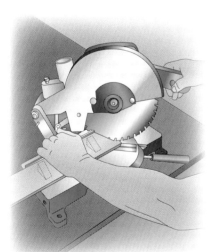

Cutting with a power mitersaw

Because the blade is round, the cut may begin not at the edge of the piece but in the middle; use a square to draw a cutline all the way across. Hold the piece firmly and keep your hand well away from the blade. Start the motor and lower the blade slowly and steadily.

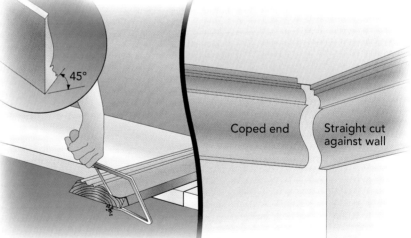

45°

Coped end | Straight cut against wall

Cutting for a coped joint

At inside corners simply bevel-cutting the two pieces may produce an imperfect joint, especially if the walls you're working with are out of square. Pros usually make a coped joint.

Cut the first piece square and install it tightly against the wall. Cut the second piece at a 45-degree miter cut, then use a coping saw to cut away the wood along the molding profile. Cut off a little more than needed to ensure a tight fit. When possible cut the coped end first, then hold the molding in place and mark to cut the other end to the correct length.

Using a router

No tool gives you the power to shape wood like a router. By choosing a bit and setting it to the proper depth, you can produce a board edge or a groove that is unique. You may even save money by milling your own molding.

Piloted bits use the edge of the board as a guide; as long as the board is straight, the routed edge will be as well. When routing in the middle of a board with other bits, however, you will find that the router jerks in a counterclockwise direction, making it hard to control. Use a clamped board (page 111) or a router guide (below right) to keep it from wandering. If you will be doing a lot of this type of work, consider buying a router table and mounting the router onto it. The table provides a flat work surface, as well as an adjustable fence for consistently accurate cuts.

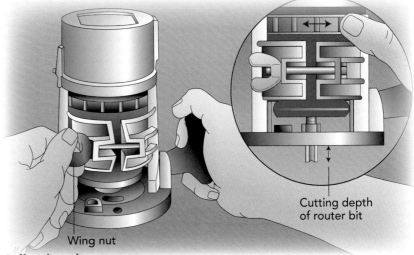

Wing nut

Cutting depth of router bit

Adjusting the router

Unplug the router and secure the bit in the chuck. To adjust the bit depth, loosen the router base around the motor. This involves turning a wing nut and adjusting the depth gauge on most models. Set the depth gauge at zero so that the bit is even with the bottom of the base. Set the router on the edge of a table and lower the bit to the desired depth. Use the depth gauge or draw a line on the edge of the table indicating depth. Tighten the nut to secure the base. Test on a scrap board.

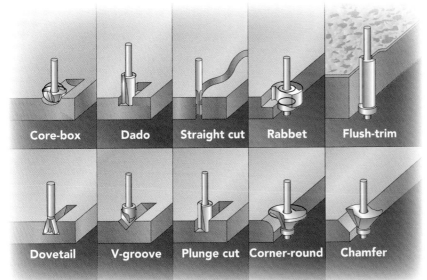

Core-box | Dado | Straight cut | Rabbet | Flush-trim

Dovetail | V-groove | Plunge cut | Corner-round | Chamfer

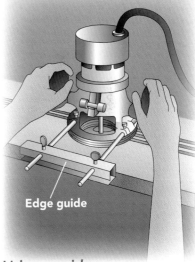

Edge guide

Choosing bits

Use a flush-trim bit, or one similar to it with a slight bevel, to finish the edges of a piece that has had a veneer of laminate glued to it. Rabbet, chamfer, and corner-round bits are all piloted so you can guide them along the edge. The ones shown have ball bearing pilots that run along the edge of the board. Some piloted bits have solid pilots that may burn the edge of the wood.

To use nonpiloted bits a guide of some sort is necessary. Cut with two or more bits, slightly offset from each other, to make unique and intricate shapes.

Router bits are very sharp and are rotating at high speed so you cannot see them while you are cutting. Keep your hands well away.

Using a guide

The guide above is an edge guide designed to rout a channel parallel to the edge of the board, one of several types of guides available. To cut circles or arcs, use a trammel-point guide, an arm with a pivot at one end. Guides are also available for cutting dovetail joints and hinge mortises. Once you've set up, you can make these cuts quickly.

Using simple joinery

Making strong, tight wood joints is basic to cabinetmaking. On these pages we show some of the easiest methods.

Boards must be cut accurately in order to be joined tightly. Hone your measuring, marking, and cutting skills before tackling joinery (see pages 96–100).

When planning a cabinet or shelf project, always take into account the joinery technique. Often the joint you choose will determine the exact length of the boards. Perhaps the most common woodworking mistake is to get confused about which board overlaps which and cut them to wrong lengths.

Visualize how the joinery method will affect the final appearance. Perhaps the joint will be hidden. If the project will be painted, then driving screws or nails in visible places is not a problem. But if it will be stained, plug the hole to enhance the cabinet's appearance.

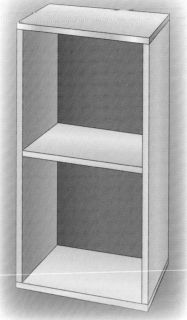

Butted ends

The simplest way to build a carcass for a cabinet or shelves is to make standard 90-degree cuts. Most professionally made cabinets use simple butt joints.

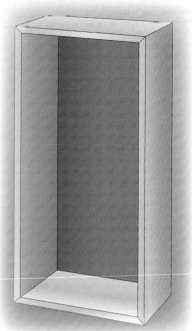

Mitered ends

For a more finished look, bevel-cut the ends so they meet in a miter joint. The wider the board, the more difficult it will be to get a perfect match.

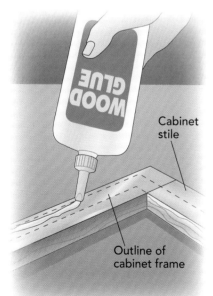

Gluing

Glue and nails work together to make a strong joint. Dry-fit the pieces, then apply an even bead of glue along the surface of one piece. If the wood is porous, brush glue onto both surfaces.

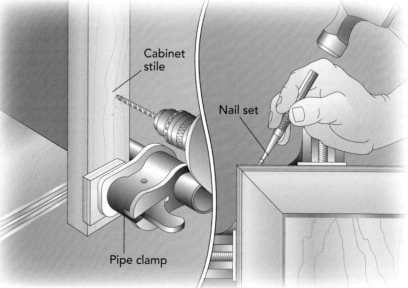

Driving and setting nails, screws

Use clamps to hold the pieces together while you fasten them.

Soon after applying the glue, drill pilot holes and drive finishing nails. Sink the heads beneath the surface with a nail set and fill the resulting hole with wood putty.

Trim head screws will grab more tightly than nails, but they will leave larger holes to fill.

To keep the corner joints snug, drill diagonal holes and drive nails or screws through each joint.

Use this inexpensive tool to drive screws as quickly as you pound nails. The sleeve, which fits into the chuck of a drill, is magnetized so that any of the small bits you insert into the end will hold onto screw heads. The bits are inexpensive, so get a good selection. The No. 2 phillips bit will be used the most often. For trim head screws you will need a No. 1 phillips bit. Add No. 2 and No. 1 slot bits, and you will be ready to drive almost any screw. When using the bit, it usually works best to place the screw head onto the bit first; that way you can drive shorter screws with one hand.

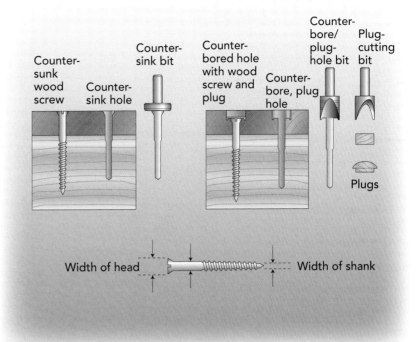

Countersinking and counterboring

A countersunk pilot hole will enable you to drive a screw head flush with the surface; a counterbored hole will let you sink the head. Combination drill bits do this quickly. Choose a bit that will allow the screw threads to grab without stressing the wood. To fill a counterbore, cut plugs out of a scrap of the same type of wood with a plug-cutting bit. Tap the plug into the hole with some glue, let dry, and sand smooth.

Hardware, wood reinforcement

The fasteners shown here can make a joint stronger or hold the pieces in place while you drill holes and drive dowels (see page 106). In casual settings that do not require a great deal of strength, they could work by themselves.

A simple flat corner iron can look dressy if you carefully mortise out the surrounding wood so that it sits perfectly flush. Small wood blocks add strength only if you drill pilot holes and fasten carefully so you don't split them. Take similar precautions when installing corner braces close to the end of a board.

Plywood makes an excellent reinforcing material because it is so hard to split. A plywood overlap secured with screws can add a surprising amount of strength; use this method where you will not see the plywood. A triangular plywood gusset adds rigidity to a corner.

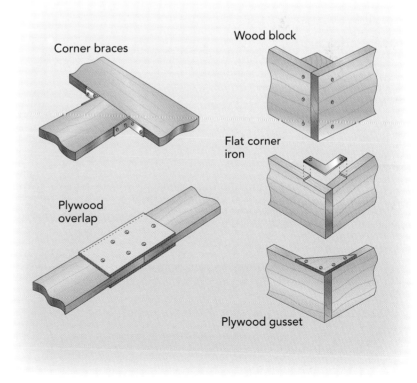

Gluing and clamping

A joint that is glued without the use of fasteners can be stronger than the wood surrounding it. For success you must use the right glue, and you must clamp it firmly in place until the glue is set.

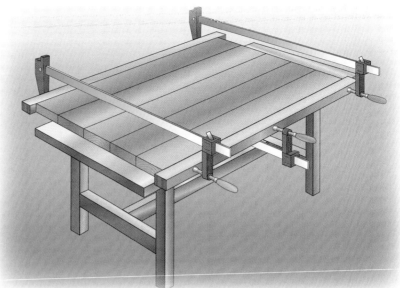

Gluing edge to edge

Gluing pieces side by side provides a surface strong enough to use as a table. The edges must be perfectly straight for good joints. Use a plane or have a shop smooth them with a jointer. Arrange the boards so the growth rings alternate (check the ends of the boards) to prevent the table from cupping with changes in humidity. Clamp very firmly.

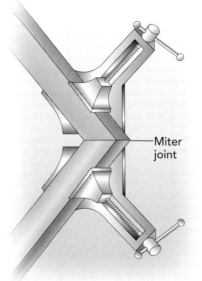

Miter joint

Miter clamp

Use this clamp for mitered joints and right-angle butt joints. It securely holds the pieces in alignment while you fasten them.

Strap clamp

Strap clamp

This will allow you to glue several joints at once, when assembling or repairing furniture, for instance.

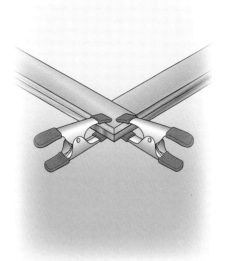

Squeeze clamps

These don't grab as securely as other clamps, but they are quick. Use for light clamping or to hold a straightedge guide for cutting.

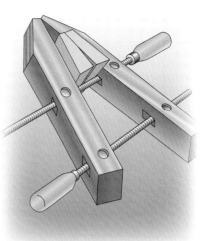

Handscrew clamps

With jaws made of wood, these are less likely than other clamps to dent the pieces. Use them to clamp pieces at almost any angle.

Squaring a cabinet

When building cabinet and shelf units, keep your layout square and framing square handy to check for square. If you drive fasteners while the pieces are out of square, you must remove the fasteners, square up the pieces, and drill new pilot holes for fasteners. (If you use thc old holes, the fasteners will pull the pieces out of square.)

Square cabinets begin with square cuts. Don't trust the ends of boards to be square (although sheet goods are trustworthy). Check each end with a square before you measure for cutting. Constantly checking for square can make it difficult to assemble cabinets, so consider making yourself a jig. This can be as simple as two pieces of 1×3 attached to your workbench, perfectly square and straight. You can then hold the pieces tight against the 1×3s as you fasten.

Check a completed unit by measuring diagonally from corner to corner. If both diagonals are equal, the structure is square.

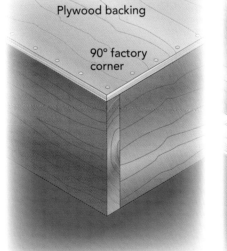

Use a piece of plywood

Plywood backing

90° factory corner

You can't trust boards to be square, but sheet goods with factory edges make excellent squares. A simple way to ensure square is to attach a piece of plywood or hardboard backing to the cabinet.

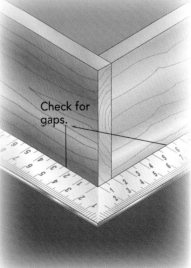

Check with a framing square

Check for gaps.

A framing (or carpenter's) square is a convenient double-duty tool for smaller projects. Use it to square up boards and to check measurements. Gaps between the square and the joint can indicate problems.

Using dowel and biscuit joinery

Professionals and serious woodworkers use complicated dovetail and mortise-and-tenon joints. For most projects—including everything in this book—simpler joints will work about as well. Inserting a reinforcement such as a dowel or a biscuit into a joint is a good practice.

Grooved Dowels

Buy ready-made dowels that are fluted, meaning they have grooves that allow space for the glue. To groove solid dowels drill a hole slightly larger than the dowel in a block of wood and drive an 8d nail into the block so it protrudes 1/16 inch into the hole. Push the dowel through the hole several times.

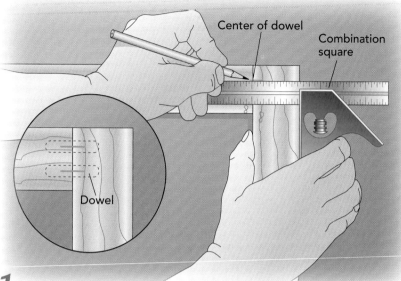

1. Mark for blind dowels.

This method will produce a joint with no visible dowel ends. Dry-fit the pieces with clamps to make sure they will fit snugly. Number the joining pieces so you remember the order of assembly. With the pieces aligned, and clamped if necessary, use a pencil and square to draw a short line spanning the joint for each dowel.

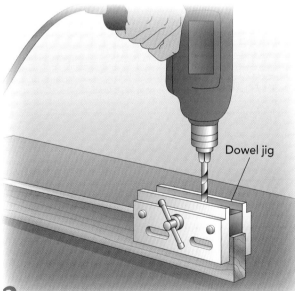

2. Drill holes with a dowel jig.

Drill holes the diameter of the dowel; 5/16-inch dowels work well for joining 1× lumber. Use a guide to drill holes, otherwise the joint will not be straight. For each hole, clamp on a dowel jig; align it with the pencil mark and center it on the thickness of the board. Set the depth gauge to drill holes slightly more than half the length of the dowels.

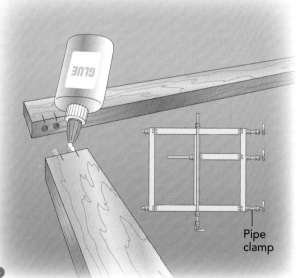

3. Glue and clamp.

If you have a number of joints to glue at the same time, be sure to have all the pieces lined up and ready to go before gluing. Squirt glue into all the holes and tap dowels into the holes on one piece. Assemble, check for square, clamp, and check for square again. Wipe away excess glue with a damp rag, or wait for it to set up a bit and scrape it off.

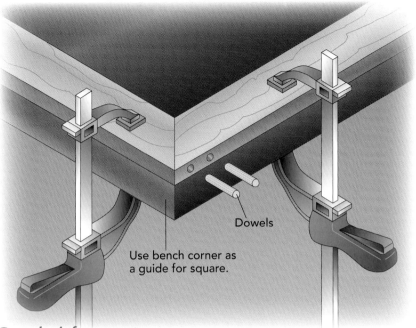

Use bench corner as a guide for square.

Dowels

Experts' Insight

Where to use dowels and biscuits

These reinforcements provide rigidity and keep joints aligned but may not add lateral strength. If the dowels or biscuits are stressed along their lengths, they can break. For instance, if two pieces are joined at right angles (below right), and downward pressure is put on the horizontal piece, dowels or biscuits can fail. However, they work great for door frames and wherever the main concern is to keep joints from pulling apart. Biscuits are easier to install. Dowels require careful measuring and drilling but are stronger.

Dowel reinforcement

This is simpler than blind doweling, but the dowel ends will show. Clamp the pieces, aligned exactly as you want them to be. (For right angles a bench corner can be a guide if you know it is accurate.) Carefully drill a hole extending through both pieces. The hole does not have to be perfectly straight, but you don't want to poke through a side. Squirt glue onto the dowels and tap them in with a mallet or a hammer and block of wood. Drive them nearly flush. After the glue dries, sand smooth.

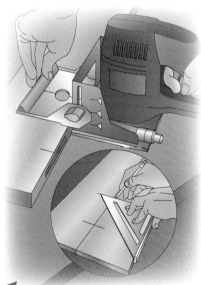

1.Mark biscuit locations.

Dry-fit the pieces and position them exactly as you want them. For each biscuit draw a short line that spans the joint.

Separate the pieces. Set the biscuit joiner to the correct depth for the size biscuit you will use. Align the joiner with the line and hold the baseplate flat as you cut.

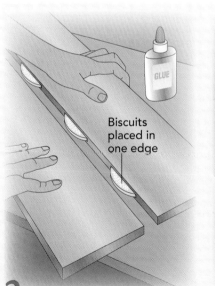

Biscuits placed in one edge

GLUE

2. Glue and clamp the joint.

Dry-fit the boards and biscuits to make sure they can fit tightly. Pull the pieces apart, squirt glue into each incision, and tap in the biscuits. Tap the second board into place, check to see that it is aligned at the ends, and clamp firm. Wipe away excess glue.

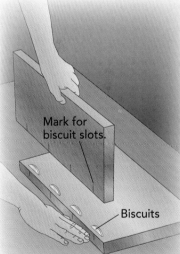

Mark for biscuit slots.

Biscuits

Assembling at a right angle

To make sure the biscuits on the vertical piece are at a perfect right angle to the horizontal piece, temporarily clamp another board to it with its top edge flush while you cut the incisions. That makes it easier to hold the baseplate flat.

Making dado, rabbet, and lap joints

Often for the sake of appearance and structural integrity, you'll want to build a cabinet or shelf with joints that use old-fashioned joinery, not just fasteners. Here are some handsome joints that, with basic carpentry tools, most novice woodworkers can manage. With a little practice you'll have a joint that is strong and pleasing to the eye.

A dado is a groove that runs across the grain of a board. The depth of a dado is about one-third the thickness of the lumber. For shelves a dado is usually cut in the shelf standard, and the butt end of a shelf fits into it. A stopped dado is a variation of the same theme, but the dado ends halfway through the standard—a feature that requires some careful chiseling. The shelf piece is notched to fit into the dado.

The depth of a dado cut is difficult to cut with precision because of imperfections in board faces and saw blades. Whenever possible, cut the dadoes first, then measure for the length of the board that will fit into them.

Rabbets are like dadoes, except that they occur at the end of a board. A rabbet cut forms a ledge that supports the other board. Use rabbet joints when building the perimeter frame of a project for a stronger and more stable joint than either a butt joint or a miter joint.

Make a full-lap joint by cutting a notch as deep as the thickness of the piece to be joined. To make a half-lap joint, notch both pieces half their thickness.

The following pages show how to make these joints using a variety of tools. Make sure your tools are sharp to make the work easier and the results better. A tablesaw is the most efficient tool. With care you can use a router, circular saw, radial-arm saw, or backsaw.

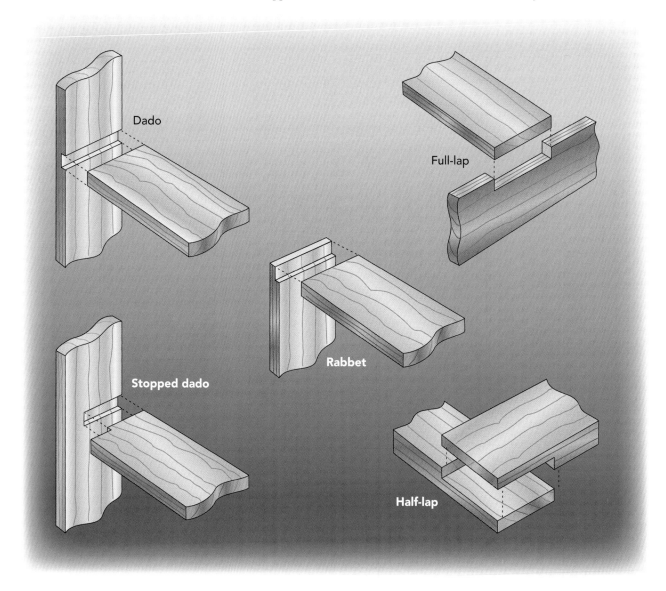

Dado

Full-lap

Rabbet

Stopped dado

Half-lap

Experts' Insight

Cutting grooves

■ Precise cuts require marking tools that make precise lines. A sharp No. 2 pencil works better than a flat carpenter's pencil. Scoring with a knife makes the thinnest line and prevents splintering outside the groove.

■ Check the thickness of the board to be inserted into the groove. Some 1× stock is slightly thicker or thinner than ¾ inch.

■ Cut test grooves on scrap wood before working on the final pieces so you can make minor width or depth adjustments without ruining an expensive piece of wood. Also, the first joints may be less than precise; practice will help.

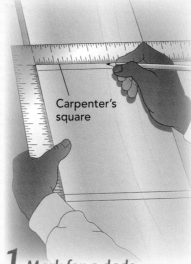

Carpenter's square

1. Mark for a dado...

Use a square and a sharp pencil or knife to draw lines indicating the outside edges of a dado or groove. Measure and mark with care. If cutting with a tablesaw, you don't need to draw lines all the way across, just starter marks. To test for accuracy before cutting, set the board that will be inserted into the groove between the lines.

or for a half-lap

Set one piece on top of the other, positioned as they will be when the lap joint is completed. Align them carefully and press down firmly. You can then mark the second board the same way. Or you can mark and cut the notch in the first board, then fit the second piece into the groove and mark it.

2. Cut with a circular saw...

For a half-lap joint, set the blade depth to half the thickness of the board. For a dado cut, set it to a third of the thickness. Use a speed square or clamped straightedge as a guide. When making each outside cut be careful not to stray outside the line. Make closely spaced cuts in the area to be removed.

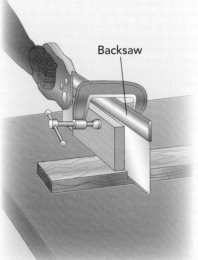

Backsaw

or with a backsaw.

Clamp a board to a backsaw for a simple and effective depth guide. Test-cut some grooves to check the depth and tighten the clamp so the board won't budge as you work. Take care to cut perpendicular to the board; the bottom edge of the depth-guide board will help you test for this.

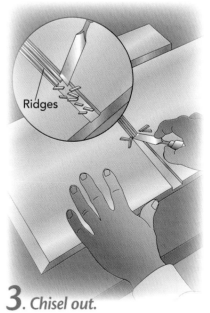

Ridges

3. Chisel out.

Use a chisel (½ to ¾ inch for dadoes and rabbets, larger for laps) to crack out the ridges. Scrape the surface with the bevel side down to remove large bumps. Finally, turn the chisel bevel-side up and scrape the groove smooth; even small bumps will ruin the joint. At all stages, keep the visible edges clean and straight.

Joining with a tablesaw or router

A tablesaw or router can make quick work of cutting long grooves, rabbets, dadoes, and notches for lap joints. However, you will need special equipment: a dado assembly for a tablesaw and a guide for a router. Mounting the router on a table would be even better.

You will not have a good view of the cuts being made with either of these tools. The router's body makes it difficult to see the bit and a tablesaw cuts the groove beneath the board. Have plenty of scrap pieces on hand so you can test to make sure the grooves will be accurate before starting.

You'll Need

TIME: Setting up may take 5 to 10 minutes. Sawing takes less than a minute per cut.
SKILLS: Measuring and marking, use of the tool.
TOOLS: Tablesaw, router, dado assembly, router guide or table.

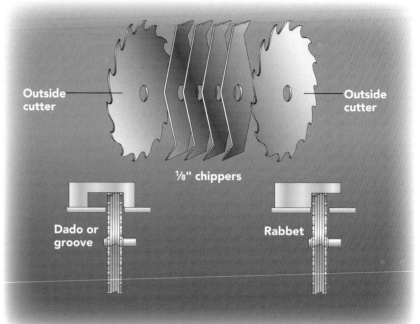

Tablesaw dado assembly

With two outside cutters and four or more ⅛-inch chippers, you can make precise grooves of various widths. You may need a throat plate with an extra-wide opening to accommodate the assembly; test by turning the blades by hand to make sure they do not scrape. A less precise alternative is an adjustable dado blade that wobbles to make a wide cut.

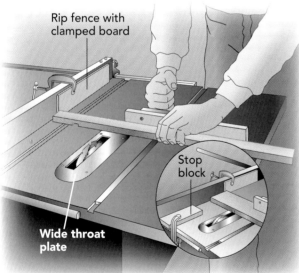

Crosscut the dado

Unplug the saw and install a dado blade and wide throat plate. Make test cuts on a scrap piece to set the depth. Make sure the miter gauge is square and use the rip fence with a clamped board to measure for the location of the dado (see page 99). For long boards attach a facing strip to the miter gauge. For stopped dadoes (page 108), clamp a stop block to the table.

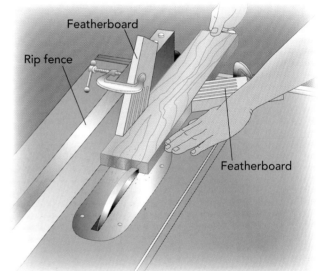

Cutting a long groove

Install the dado assembly and clamp the rip fence so it is parallel to the blade. Clamp one or two featherboards to protect against kickback. Test on scrap pieces until the cuts are correctly positioned and at the proper depth. Caution: The blade is not visible sometimes. Keep your hands well away from the blade. Use a push stick (see the opposite page) when ending a cut.

110 *Basic skills*

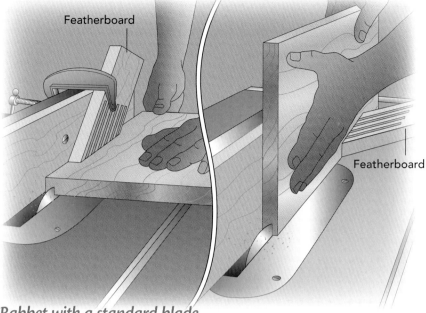

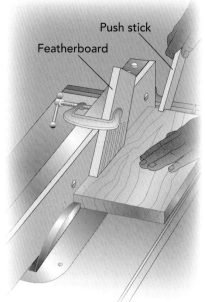

Rabbet with a standard blade

Adjust for the depth of the rabbet and test on a scrap piece. Attach a piece of wood to the side of the rip fence, and adjust it so the saw cuts on the waste side of the cutline. Clamp a featherboard to the fence and run the piece through. Remove the featherboard and make the second cut by holding the piece vertically against the fence. Test your setup on scrap pieces and make adjustments as needed. (With rabbets as deep as they are wide, you won't need to adjust the blade or the fence.)

Rabbet with a dado blade

Unplug the saw and install the dado-cutting assembly. Slide the rip fence nearly against the blades and clamp a featherboard onto the fence. Test-cut scraps until you have the correct depth and width, then cut the parts.

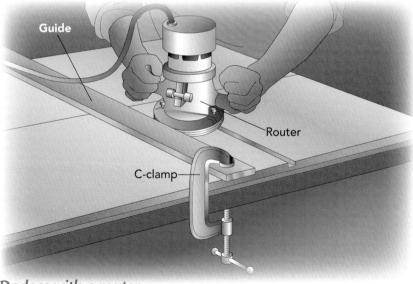

Dadoes with a router

A router with a straight bit quickly cuts a groove. Make sure the guide is tightly clamped and firmly press the tool against the guide as you cut; a moment's lapse can make a crooked groove. Always push or pull the router against the rotation of the blade—the direction of most resistance. If you move with the rotation of the blade, the router will probably skate away. Hone your techniques on scraps.

Making a cabinet door

There are two basic types of cabinet doors: A panel door is more complicated to make and requires a tablesaw; a slab door is a single piece of wood, usually plywood. Slab doors are usually edged with trim for a neater appearance and to prevent warping. In addition to selecting a door style, decide how the door will fit in the cabinet (see page 114). A flush door fits inside the cabinet frame and must be sized so there is an even ⅛-inch gap all around. An inset door has a rabbeted edge around its perimeter that covers the frame. An overlay door fits entirely over the frame and is the easiest to make.

You'll Need

TIME: 2 hours for a panel door; or a half hour for a trimmed slab.
SKILLS: Measuring and cutting.
TOOLS: Tablesaw, dado assembly, power or hand mitersaw, drill.

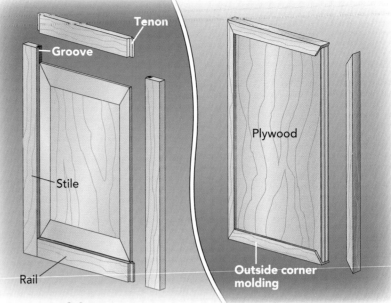

Two types of doors

A panel door has two horizontal rails and two vertical stiles. All four pieces have a groove into which the panel fits. Each rail has a tenon on each end that fits into the groove of the stile. The panel could be a flat piece of thin plywood, but a more attractive option is to bevel the edges of a wide 1× board.

The slab door shown has been trimmed with outside corner molding around the perimeter. This is a quick and easy way to dress up a door.

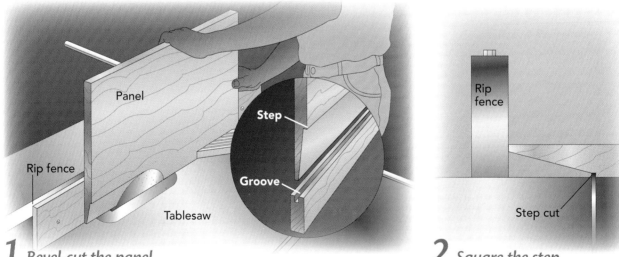

1. Bevel-cut the panel.

If the panel will be wider than 11¼ inches (the width of a 1×12), clamp and glue pieces edge-to-edge (see page 104). Fasten a piece of 1×6 or 1×8 to the rip fence to keep the workpiece from wobbling while you work. Adjust the blade so the bottom edge of the bevel will be just thick enough to fit into the groove you will make in the rails and stiles (see Step 3 on page 113). To give the panel a "step," adjust so the top edge of the cut will be ⅛ inch below the face of the board. If you don't want a step, raise the blade to cut through. Remove the blade guard and keep your hands well away from the blade. Bevel-cut all four edges.

2. Square the step.

If you chose to have a stepped bevel, square the blade and adjust it down so it cuts only ⅛ inch deep. Align the fence so that the blade will cut only the top edge of the bevel and square it up. Test with scraps; this calls for precise adjustment. Run all four sides of the panel through the saw.

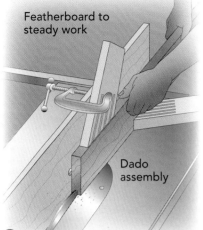

Featherboard to steady work

Dado assembly

3. Groove the rails and stiles.

Install a dado assembly (see page 110) that cuts the same width as the thickness of the door panel at the perimeter. Set the cutting depth to $\frac{1}{2}$ inch. Test cut on a scrap to make sure the panel will fit the groove snugly. With the 1×6 or 1×8 clamped to the fence, adjust the fence so the blade will cut in the exact center of a board edge. (Test for this by cutting a groove, turning the piece around, and cutting again.) Cut a groove on the inside edge of all rails and stiles.

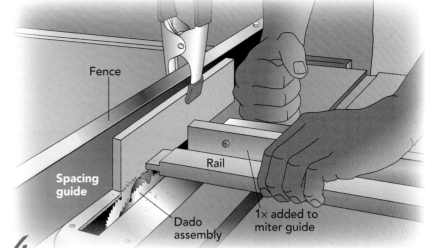

Fence

Rail

Spacing guide

Dado assembly

1× added to miter guide

4. Cut tenons.

Each rail must have a tenon on both ends. Make the tenon $\frac{1}{2}$ inch long and as thick as the groove width. This means that the rail itself should be 1 inch longer than the distance between stiles, the same as the width of the panel.

Set the dado cutting depth to half the board's thickness minus half the thickness of the tenon. Attach a straight piece of 1× scrap to the miter guide so you can hold the rail firmly as you cut. Clamp a scrap

piece to the front end of the rip fence to use as a spacing guide (see page 99). Adjust the fence so it positions the rail to cut a $\frac{1}{2}$-inch-wide tenon. Cut one side of the tenon, flip the board over, and cut the other.

Experiment on scrap pieces to achieve the precise blade height and the exact width adjustment so that the tenon fits snugly into a stile groove. Take your time, test your setup, and get it right: This is the step that determines appearance.

Bar clamp

Glue rail tenons only.

5. Clamp and glue.

Sand any saw marks on the panel. Dry-fit the pieces to make sure they fit tightly. Remove the stiles and apply glue to the rail tenons. (Don't glue the panel into the groove; it must be allowed to expand and contract with changes in humidity without stressing the stiles and rail.) Clamp and let dry.

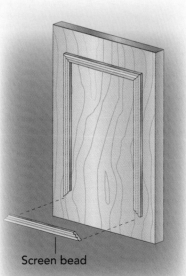

Screen bead

Achieve a raised look

You can dress up a new or old slab door by installing moldings. Two bands of molding, running either vertically or horizontally, add elegance to any slab door. Or miter-cut four pieces of thin molding, such as fluted screen bead, to form a frame on the door. Even chair rail can be applied for an ornamental look.

Plan all the doors at the same time: Horizontal pieces should all be at the same height, and the distance between molding and door edge should be the same for all doors.

Installing hinged doors

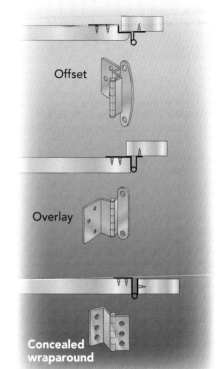

Offset

Overlay

Concealed wraparound

Most cabinet projects call for unobtrusive hinges that, if visible at all, meld with any decor. Of the types commonly available, Euro-style hinges (see page 87) are the most expensive and are entirely concealed. Overlay and offset hinges (right) are mostly hidden, with only the smaller hinge leaf visible. If you have flush doors, a concealed wraparound hinge (right) will be nearly invisible. Surface-mount decorative hinges are also available for flush-fitting doors.

When building new cabinets, install hinges and knobs last, after the doors and drawers are painted or finished. If you want to dress up old cabinets by painting or refinishing, remove the hinges and knobs first. (It is nearly impossible to paint around hinges, and removing them takes surprisingly little time.)

A neat installation of smoothly functioning hinges requires care and patience. All the hinges in a row of cabinets should be at the same height. If a change of height is required, the change should be consistent. Also, cabinet hinges determine the height and angle of doors. If a hinge is installed even $1/16$ inch out of alignment, the door will be noticeably out of line with the other doors. If the hinges are not adjustable—and most, except Euro-style hinges, are not—it will be difficult to move one slightly. Work systematically with attention to detail.

You will find yourself often alternating between drilling pilot holes and driving screws. Have two drills on hand, one with a pilot bit and one equipped with a magnetic sleeve and screwdriver bit. Cordless drills make this much easier. Most hinge screws call for a No. 1 phillips bit; the more common No. 2 bit is too big to fit the screws properly and makes driving them difficult.

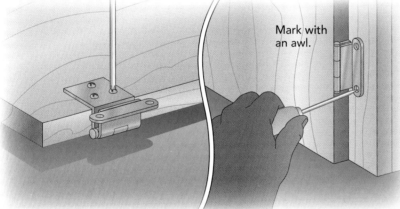

Mark with an awl.

Installing an overlay hinge

With the door facedown place the hinges about 2 inches from the top and bottom; use a spacer or jig to ensure that all the hinges in a group of cabinets are placed in identical positions. Drill pilot holes in the exact center of each hole and drive the screws.

Next, position the door on the cabinet exactly as it will be when hung using spacers or clamp-on guides. Have a helper hold it while you work. Mark for the pilot holes using an awl, then remove the door to drill the pilot holes. If you feel confident that the door is firmly and correctly in place, drill the pilot holes through the hinge holes and drive the screws in the same operation.

Experts' Insight
Always drill pilot holes

Constantly alternating between drilling pilot holes and driving screws may seem tedious, and you will be tempted to skip an occasional pilot hole and just drive in the screw. Resist that temptation. Though a hinge screw is small, it can easily crack a cabinet stile. A cracked stile must be glued and clamped, a time-consuming process. Also, pilot holes make it much easier to drive the screws straight; crooked screws look unprofessional. See page 124 for hole sizes.

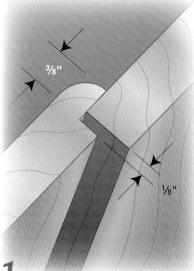

1. Measure for an inset door.

An inset or lipped door is ¼ inch larger on all sides than the opening. The rabbet running all around the door is ⅜ inch wide, giving a clearance of ⅛ inch between the inside of the rabbet and the cabinet. You must measure carefully to get a good fit.

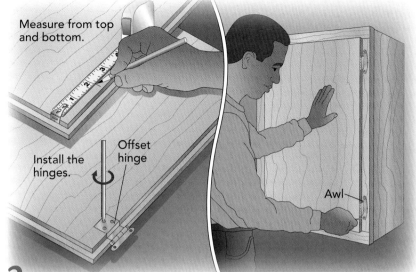

2. Install an offset hinge.

Place the door facedown and install the hinges about 2 inches from the top and bottom. Use the same spacing for all the doors.

The key is to center the inset door in the opening. Place ⅛-inch hardboard spacers on the bottom and one side of the opening. Set the door on the spacers (carefully, since you won't be able to see the spacers). Align the door precisely; you may have to pull it away from a spacer slightly. Mark for pilot holes with an awl, or drill pilot holes through the hinge holes and drive the screws.

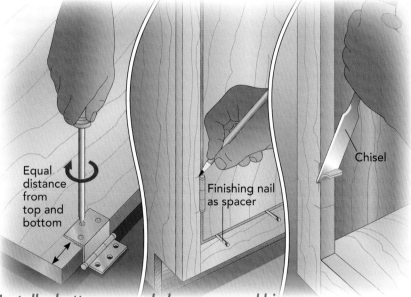

Install a butt or concealed wraparound hinge

For flush doors measure an equal distance from top and bottom, as for an overlay hinge (see opposite page). Install the wraparound hinge on the inside of the door.

For a butt hinge use a chisel and knife to cut a mortise and install one leaf of the hinge in the mortise. Use two finishing nails as spacers and center the door in the opening so that there is a consistent ⅛-inch gap all around. Use a sharp pencil to mark the top and bottom of the hinge. Remove the door and cut a mortise as thick as the hinge leaf. Position the hinges, mark and drill pilot holes, then drive the screws.

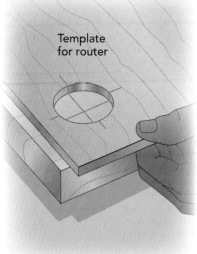

1. Drill for concealed hinge.

Drill the recess hole with a Forstner bit (below), or make a template and cut it with a router. The hole in the template must be large enough to allow use of a guide bushing in the router base.

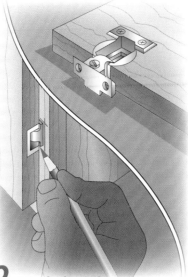

2. Mark the stile.

Insert the hinge in the door, drill pilot holes, and drive the screws. Position the door against the face frame. While a helper holds it in the correct position, mark the location of the hinges on the stile.

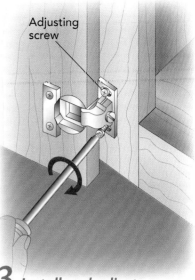

3. Install and adjust.

With the door open have the helper hold the hinges against the marks on the stile. Carefully try the movement of the door until it fits smoothly. Center the adjusting screws in the slots provided. Loosen or tighten the screws to adjust the door position.

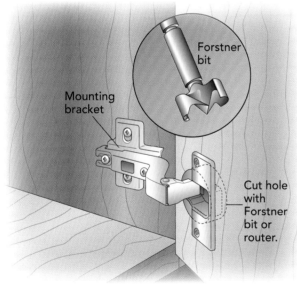

Euro-style hinge

This type of hinge can be used for an overlay or flush door. It is the easiest hinge to adjust, allowing you to move it up and down, in and out. One side fits into a recess hole in the door, which you can drill with a Forstner bit or cut with a router. The arm slides onto a mounting bracket. To install it, first mount the hinge in the recess hole. Install the mounting bracket onto the inside of the cabinet, then slide the hinge arm onto the mounting bracket.

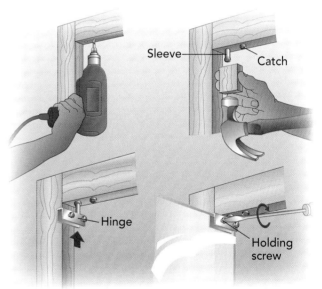

Glass-door hinge

Glass doors are always flush, fitting inside the cabinet. To mount the type shown, drill a pair of holes (usually ¼-inch) near the edge of the top rail and another pair near the edge of the bottom rail. Tap a sleeve into the hole nearest the end and a catch into the other hole. Slip hinges into the sleeves, fit the glass door into the hinges, adjust the door so it fits inside the opening, and tighten the holding screws on the hinges.

Installing catches and pulls

Fastening cabinet catches calls for no special skills, but you must have patience. You will often be working in tight places, and you might not have enough room to drill and drive screws straight.

Position a catch as close as possible to the handle or pull to reduce stress to the hinges. In most cases the catch is mounted to the cabinet and the strike to the door. Usually you should mount base-cabinet pulls and catches near the top of the door and wall-cabinet pulls and catches near the bottom of the door. A magnetic screwdriver or a magnetic sleeve holds the screw on the bit, speeding the job.

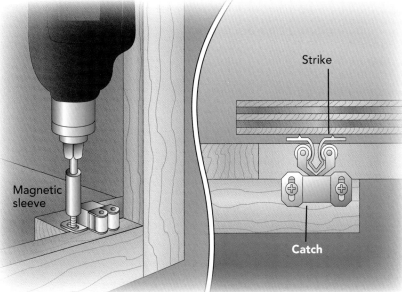

You'll Need

TIME: About 15 minutes for an average catch.
SKILLS: Drilling pilot holes and driving screws, measuring.
TOOLS: Drill, screwdriver.

Install catches

To mount any kind of catch, attach the catch first, then the strike. Drill pilot holes to avoid splitting the wood and to ensure that the screws go in straight.

Whenever possible use the catch itself to help with marking. For a spring catch like the one shown above, attach the catch and insert the strike into it. Close the door firmly. The marking points on the front of the strike will make indentations in the door showing you where to mount the strike.

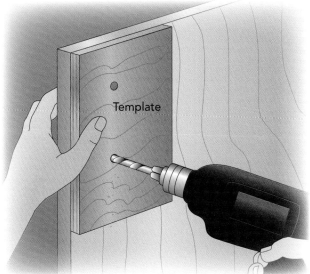

Make a template to drill for door pulls

All the door pulls in a group of cabinets should be at the same height or else the cabinets will look unprofessional. It is easy to achieve this uniformity if you use a template like the one shown. Drill holes in a piece of wood spaced where you want them on each door. Hold the template with its edges flush with the door edges, then drill the holes.

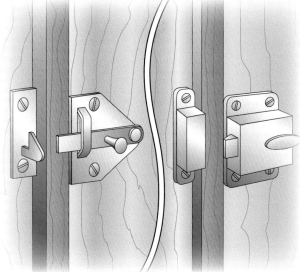

Install a decorative latch

These latches usually work for flush doors only. Installing them is simple. With the door closed, position the latch with its edge flush with the edge of the door, drill pilot holes, and drive screws. Close the door and place the strike on the cabinet so that the latch can close on it. Drill pilot holes and drive screws to install the strike.

Installing sliding doors

Purchase metal tracks for sliding doors made of ¾-inch plywood. The top track has deeper channels, the other track goes on the bottom. If the cabinet is faced with a frame, fit the tracks against the back side of the frame. If not, position them about ¼ inch in from the front edge of the cabinet.

Protruding door pulls would get in the way as one door slides past the other. Instead, drill holes for pulls. Position the holes about ¾ inch from the outside edge of each door, centered vertically. Drill through with a hole saw and sand the edges. Or drill partway through with a Forstner bit and tap in a round metal door pull.

Fit the door panels—the rear one first—by lifting them up into the top track and dropping them into the bottom track.

Upper track is deeper.

Hole saw

Lower track has shallow guides.

Building and installing a drawer

For drawers 24 inches square or smaller, make the sides from ½-inch plywood and the bottom from ¼-inch. Usually the facepiece is ¾-inch stock to match the cabinet door thickness.

Manufactured drawers often use complicated dovetail joints, but the rabbet-and-groove joints shown are easier to construct and are strong enough for most uses.

Make drawers at least 2 inches shorter than the depth of the cabinet and ¼ inch smaller than the height and width of the opening (not including the facepiece).

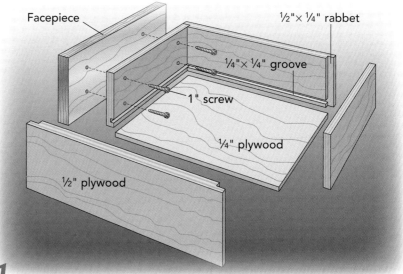

Facepiece

½"× ¼" rabbet

¼"× ¼" groove

1" screw

¼" plywood

½" plywood

You'll Need

TIME: A couple of hours to make one drawer.
SKILLS: Cutting grooves, rabbets; fastening nails, screws.
TOOLS: Circular saw, drill, tape measure, framing square.

1. *Cut the parts.*

Cut the back and front pieces to ½ inch less than the total width of the drawer; cut the sidepieces to the total length. Use a tablesaw, radial-arm saw, or circular saw to cut grooves in the sides and front, ¼ inch up from the bottom edge. Cut ½-inch rabbets ¼-inch-deep in both ends of the sidepieces. Cut the facepiece larger than the front. Assemble the front and sides and measure for a bottom that fits in the grooves and extends to the back ends of the sidepieces.

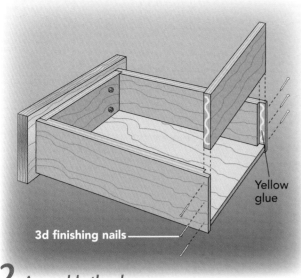

3d finishing nails

Yellow glue

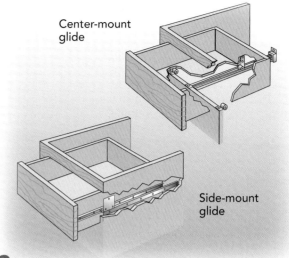

Center-mount glide

Side-mount glide

2. Assemble the drawer.

Align the facepiece and attach it with four 1-inch general-purpose screws through the front piece and into the facepiece. Rip-cut the backpiece so its top is flush with the top of the sidepieces when it sits on the bottom piece. Squeeze glue onto the rabbets and the ends of the front and back pieces and assemble the four outside pieces. Slide the bottom in, but do not apply glue to the grooves. Check for square and drive 3d finishing nails through the rabbet joints and up through the bottom into the backpiece.

3. Choose drawer glides.

Side-mount drawer glides, which are more expensive than center-mount drawer glides with side rollers, operate more smoothly, last longer, and can handle heavier loads. Inexpensive models use plastic rollers; better-quality side-mounts feature ball-bearing rollers. They are available in lengths from 12 to 28 inches. Choose glides that are an inch or so shorter than the length of the drawer.

Experts' Insight

Drawer tips

■ Every drawer must be square. If it's out of square, the face will not rest flush against the cabinet front, and the drawer may rub against the cabinet sides.
■ Do not attach the drawer bottom with glue or nails anywhere except at the rear piece. Otherwise, it will put stress on the rabbet joints when it expands and contracts with changes in humidity.
■ Keep the drawer dry. Tossing in wet silverware, for instance, can eventually cause warping. For protection, line the bottom of the drawer with shelf paper.

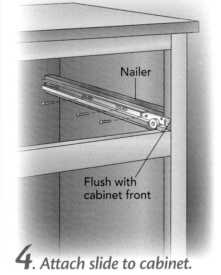

Nailer

Flush with cabinet front

4. Attach slide to cabinet.

You may need to install a nailer to support the slide. Drill pilot holes and drive screws to attach the glides so they are level, the front edges flush with the front of the cabinet.

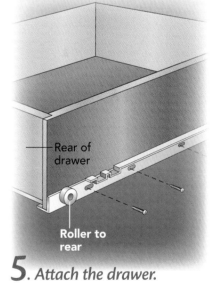

Rear of drawer

Roller to rear

5. Attach the drawer.

Install the other pieces of the glide to the sides of the drawer. The rollers go to the rear. Slip the rollers into the cabinet-mounted glide pieces and test for smooth operation.

Edging and finishing

Once you've finished building a project, you can complete the finishing touches—edging, filling holes, sanding, and staining or painting. The square corners and tight joints will not be noticed if the wood surface looks unfinished. Conversely, an imperfectly constructed cabinet becomes respectable with careful sanding and staining.

Tools for finishing are simple: A putty knife, a sanding block (or an electric sander if you are doing a lot of work), a paintbrush, and a small pile of rags may be all you need.

Remove all visible glue before finishing. Either wipe excess glue with a damp rag while it is wet or let it partially harden and scrape most of it away with a putty knife. After you have used one of these methods, wait until the residual glue dries, then sand it away.

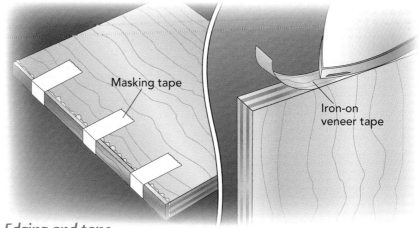

Edging and tape

Plywood edges are unattractive. Most edges are covered during the course of building shelves and cabinets, but often some remain exposed. It's easier to cover an edge than to finish or paint it.

Shelf edging and screen molding are ¾ inch wide and ¼ inch thick. If you install them with finishing nails, you will have nailheads to set and

fill, and you may split the molding. Instead, apply glue and then tape the molding tight until the glue sets.

Or purchase iron-on veneer tape. Use scissors to cut a piece a bit longer than needed. Press it in place with a hot iron until the glue melts. Wait a couple of minutes, then trim the waste with a knife and sand the edges lightly.

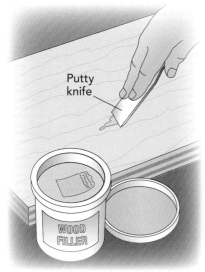

Filling holes

Use colored wood filler after staining, or use stainable putty before staining. Push the filler into holes with your finger, then scrape with a putty knife. Either wipe away the excess with a damp rag or allow the putty to dry, then sand it smooth.

Sanding

Attach sandpaper to a sanding block rather than using a loose piece of sandpaper. Sand with medium pressure—don't force it—and move in the direction of the grain. Examine your work from various angles and feel the surface.

Lint-free rag

Apply stain.

Choose a penetrating stain and experiment with scrap pieces of the same wood species before staining your project. Apply heavily with a brush, wait a few minutes, then wipe with a lint-free rag (not a paper towel). Make it darker by applying and wiping stain again; lighten by rubbing with a cloth moistened with water or thinner. After staining, apply clear finish (see chart, below).

Choosing and applying clear finishes

Type	Characteristics and Application Tips
Oil-base polyurethane	Hard and long-lasting but tends to yellow with time; yellowing will not be noticeable if it is applied over a stain. Apply with a bristle brush.
Water-base polyurethane	Not as durable as oil-base but it doesn't yellow. Apply with a synthetic brush.
Oil finish	Not as durable as polyurethane but many prefer its appearance, and it is easier to repair. Apply several coats. Danish oil, which is available mixed with stain, is the easiest to apply.
Varnish	An older product that has oils and resins. Spar varnish stays flexible and is suitable for outdoor use. Apply with a bristle brush.
Shellac	An alcohol-based product that is thick and dries quickly. Easily marred by water or alcohol. Apply with a bristle brush.
Lacquer	Used mostly by professionals, lacquer produces a silky surface but is difficult to use. Apply many coats with an ox-hair brush.

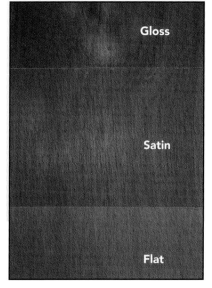

Gloss

Satin

Flat

Several types of finishes

Different sheens of clear finishes subtly alter the look of stained wood. When painting, use semigloss or gloss enamel for easy cleaning.

Glossary

For words not listed here, or for more about those that are, refer to the index, pages 125–127.

Actual dimensions. The true dimensions of lumber after milling and drying. *See Nominal dimension.*

Bevel-cut. An angle cut through the thickness of a piece of wood.

Biscuit joiner. A power tool used to cut incisions in lumber into which flat, football-shaped wooden biscuits are glued.

Blind dado. A channel cut across the grain or width of a workpiece that stops short of one or both edges.

Building codes. Community ordinances governing the manner in which a building may be constructed or modified. Most codes are primarily concerned with fire safety and health, with separate sections relating to electrical, plumbing, and structural work.

Butt joint. The joint formed by two pieces of material when fastened end-to-end, end-to-face, or end-to-edge.

Carcass. The boxlike outer body or framework of a cabinet or shelving unit.

Casing. Trimming around a door, window, or other opening.

Cleat. A length of board attached to strengthen a structure or support another part.

Counterbore. To drive a screw below the surface of the surrounding wood. The void created is filled later with putty or is plugged.

Countersink. To drive the head of a nail or screw so that the top is flush with the surface of the surrounding wood.

Cove. A concave form, as in the face of a style of molding.

Crosscut. To saw a piece of lumber perpendicular to its length and/or its grain.

Dado joint. A joint formed when the end of one member fits into a groove cut partway through the face of another.

Dowel. A piece of small-diameter wood rod, often used to reinforce joints.

Doweling jig. A device that clamps onto a workpiece edge or end and aids in accurately locating and drilling holes for dowels.

Drywall. A basic interior building material consisting of sheets of pressed gypsum faced with heavy paper on both sides. Also known as wallboard, gypsum board, plasterboard, and sheetrock.

Edging. Strips of wood or veneer used to cover the edges of plywood or boards.

End grain. The ends of wood fibers that are exposed at the ends of boards.

Face frame. The front surface of a cabinet or chest of drawers. Constructed of stiles and rails, it frames the openings for doors or drawers.

Filler. A pastelike compound used to hide surface imperfections in wood. Another type—pore filler—levels the surface of wood that has a coarse grain.

Flush. On the same plane as, or level with, an adjoining piece or surface.

Grit. The abrasive material bonded to a piece of sandpaper. Grits are designated by numbers, such as 120-grit and 240-grit. The higher the number the finer the abrasive.

Hardwood. Lumber that comes from leaved, deciduous trees, such as oak and maple.

Joist. Horizontal framing members that support a floor or ceiling or both.

Kerf. The void created by the blade of a saw as it cuts partially through a piece of material.

Laminate. A hard plastic decorative veneer applied to cabinets and shelves. Can refer to a material formed by building up layers, as in plywood or to the process of applying a decorative laminate to a surface, such as a countertop.

Lap joint. The joint formed when one member overlaps another.

Layout. A plan, often sketched on the wall or floor, showing where cabinets or shelves will be located.

Ledger. A horizontal strip (usually lumber) that's used to provide support for the ends or edges of other members.

Level. The condition that exists when any type of surface is at true horizontal. Also a tool used to determine level.

Linear foot. The simple length of a board or piece of molding (in contrast to board foot, which refers to volume).

Load-bearing wall. A wall that supports a wall or roof section on the floor above. Do not cut or remove a stud in a load-bearing wall without proper alternative support. *See Partition wall.*

MDF (Medium Density Fiberboard). Made of very fine wood chips, this material is available in sheets and as 12- and 16-inch-wide pieces often used for shelving.

Miter joint. The joint formed when two members meet that have been cut at the same angle.

Molding. A strip of wood, usually thin and narrow, sometimes having a decorative profile, used to cover exposed edges or as decoration.

Mortise. A shallow cutout in a board, usually used to recess hardware such as hinges.

Nominal dimension. The stated size of a piece of lumber, such as a 2×4 or a 1×12. The actual dimension is smaller.

On center (OC). The distance from the center of one regularly spaced framing member or hole to the center of the next.

1× (2×). Refers to nominal 1- or 2-inch thick lumber of any width, length, or type of wood. The actual lumber dimensions are $3/4$ inch and $1\frac{1}{2}$ inches thick, respectively.

Particleboard. Sheetgoods made from compressed wood chips and glue.

Partition wall. Unlike a load-bearing wall, a partition supports no structure above it and can therefore be removed.

Pilot hole. A small hole drilled into a wooden member to avoid splitting the wood when driving a screw or nail.

Plumb. The condition that exists for a part of a structure that is truly vertical.

Rabbet. A step-shaped cut made along the edge of a piece of wood, often used to join parts of a structure.

Rails. Horizontal pieces of a door or cabinet face frame.

Rip. To saw lumber or sheet goods parallel to the grain pattern.

Roughing-in. The framing stage of a carpentry project. This framework is later concealed in the finishing stages.

Rout. To shape edges or cut grooves, using a router.

Scratch sealer. A protective, usually clear, coating applied to wood or metal.

Scribe. To use a geometry compass or scrap of wood to transfer the shape or dimension of an object to a piece of wood to be cut.

Setting nails. Driving the heads of nails slightly below the surface of the wood.

Shim. A thin strip or wedge of wood or other material used to fill a gap between two adjoining components or to help establish level or plumb.

Sliding door track. A set of grooves or runners along the front of a cabinet at the top and bottom that holds sliding cabinet doors in place and permits them to slide.

Spacer. A piece of finished wood or other material used to fill in the space at the end of a run of cabinets.

Square. The condition that exists when one surface lies at a 90-degree angle to another. Also, a tool used to determine when a corner is square.

Stiles. Vertical members of a door assembly or cabinet facing.

Stringer. The main structural member of a stairway.

Stud finder. An electronic or magnetic tool that locates studs within a finished wall.

Studs. Vertical 2×4 or 2×6 framing members spaced at regular intervals within a wall.

Template. A pattern to follow when re-creating a precise shape.

Toe-kick. Indentation at the bottom of a floor-based cabinet. Also known as toe space.

Toenail. To drive a nail at an angle, so as to hold together two pieces of material.

Veneer. A thin layer of decorative wood laminated to the surface of a more common wood.

Veneer tape. A ribbon of reinforced wood veneer applied to edges of plywood or other sheet goods with glue or heat-sensitive adhesive.

Wall anchor. A fastener such as a toggle bolt or lead insert used to secure objects to hollow walls or masonry walls.

Warp. Any of several lumber defects caused by uneven shrinkage of wood cells.

Reference

Holes for screws

Wood screws		Pilot hole		Deck/drywall screws (drill both parts)	
Screw size	Shank hole	Softwood	Hardwood	Softwood	Hardwood
2	3/32"	1/16"	1/16"		
3	7/64"	1/16"	1/16"		
4	7/64"	1/16"	5/64"	1/16"	5/64"
5	1/8"	1/16"	5/64"		
6	9/64"	5/64"	3/32"	3/32"	7/64"
7	5/32"	3/32"	7/64"		
8	5/32"	3/32"	7/64"	7/64"	1/8"
9	11/64"	7/64"	1/8"		
10	3/16"	7/64"	1/8"	1/8"	9/64"
12	7/32"	1/8"	9/64"		

Hardwood sizes

Quarter size	Thickness (surfaced)
4/4	13/16"
5/4	1 1/16"
6/4	1 5/16"
7/4	1 1/2"
8/4	1 3/4"
10/4	2 1/4"
12/4	2 3/4"
16/4	3 3/4"

Nails

Common, box, finishing, and casing nails of the same penny (d) size are the same length, but have different diameters. Thinner box nails are less likely to split wood than common nails; drill pilot holes for nails that are near the ends of boards to minimize splitting. Cement-coated (CC) box nails hold best. Higher wire gauge numbers indicate smaller diameters.

		Pilot hole diameter		
Size	Length	Box nail	Finishing nail	Depth
3d	1 1/4"	1/16"	1/16"	3/4" deep
4d	1 1/2"	1/16"	1/16"	1" deep
6d	2"	5/64"	5/64"	1 5/16" deep
8d	2 1/2"	3/32"	5/64"	1 5/8" deep
10d	3"	7/64"	3/32"	2" deep
16d	3 1/2"	7/64"	—	2 1/4" deep

Board feet

A board-foot is one square foot one inch thick. Here's how to calculate it, using an 8-foot-long 2×4 as an example:

- Multiply thickness times width, using nominal dimensions. 2×4=8

- Multiply that result times the length, in feet or inches.
  In feet, 8×8=64
  In inches, 8×96=768

- Divide the result by 12 (if the length is in feet) or 144 (if the length is in inches).
  64÷12=5.33 board-feet
  768÷144=5.33 board-feet

Glues for woodworking

PVA (polyvinyl acetate)	White glue. Strong, not waterproof. Long open (working) time. Joints must fit well. Corrodes steel.
Aliphatic resin	Yellow glue. Strong, grabs fast. Moisture resistant, not waterproof. Corrodes steel. Popular wood glue.
Modified PVA	Waterproof yellow glue. Withstands weather exposure, not submersion. Generally similar to yellow glue.
Liquid hide glue	Easier-to-use version of traditional hot hide glue. Long open time. Heat and moisture weaken bond.
Polyurethane	Expands in joint as it cures, so must be clamped. Strong, waterproof. Bonds wood, metal, plastics.
Cyanoacrylate ester	Bonds instantly to many materials (including skin). Strong, not shock resistant. Requires tight joint.
Epoxy	Strong, water-resistant for many materials. Mix for use. Comes in five-minute or longer-setting varieties.
Construction adhesive	Often sold in caulking-gun tubes. Thick, strong. Formulations for many construction purposes.

Index